The Groom's Arrival

The Ancient Hebrew Wedding Tradition and the Return of Christ

JOHN COOPER

WestBow
PRESS

Copyright © 2011 John Cooper

All rights reserved. No part of this book may be used or reproduced by any means, graphic, electronic, or mechanical, including photocopying, recording, taping or by any information storage retrieval system without the written permission of the publisher except in the case of brief quotations embodied in critical articles and reviews.

Scripture taken from the New King James Version. Copyright 1979, 1980, 1982 by Thomas Nelson, inc. Used by permission. All rights reserved.

WestBow Press books may be ordered through booksellers or by contacting:

WestBow Press
A Division of Thomas Nelson
1663 Liberty Drive
Bloomington, IN 47403
www.westbowpress.com
1-(866) 928-1240

Because of the dynamic nature of the Internet, any web addresses or links contained in this book may have changed since publication and may no longer be valid. The views expressed in this work are solely those of the author and do not necessarily reflect the views of the publisher, and the publisher hereby disclaims any responsibility for them.

Any people depicted in stock imagery provided by Thinkstock are models, and such images are being used for illustrative purposes only.

Certain stock imagery © Thinkstock.

ISBN: 978-1-4497-1751-3 (sc)
ISBN: 978-1-4497-1752-0 (hc)
ISBN: 978-1-4497-1750-6 (e)

Library of Congress Control Number: 2011929576

Printed in the United States of America

WestBow Press rev. date: 7/12/2011

Preface

Looking for treasure? Jesus said,
"Lay up for yourselves treasures in heaven ..." (Matthew 6:20[1])

When you start to read the book of Revelation, what is the first thought that pops into your mind? Are you looking for the blessing that you'll receive, or, do you read it with trepidation, as you heed the warning to not add to or take away from its meaning? Are you fearful of the future events that it portrays, and do your first thoughts turn to the tribulation and judgments that will come? I've got good news for you! There is much "treasure" in the pages of Revelation, which bring a blessing that will draw you closer to Him.

Did you ever use Cliff's Notes to help you comprehend the content of a book? Jesus, in His Olivet Discourse, is giving us His notes on Revelation. Chapter 1, verse 3 tells us that it is good for us to read Revelation, because we will receive a special blessing. Revelation is God's final chapter to His "love story." As you read The Groom's Arrival, you will gain insight into the ancient Hebrew wedding tradition and how it helps you put the pieces of the story into a proper order. The Groom's Arrival draws from the rich symbolism of the ancient tradition and interweaves it with the scriptures that surround Christ's return. The message of the study is one of hope, as we await the glorious promises of Christ's arrival.

More important than my written words in this book are the 1,000 scripture reverences and the "hidden treasure" each reader will discover for himself. Read as an explorer who seeks to understand God's love story. God has always sought to reveal to us His Word and purpose, as He seeks to bless a people and to call them His own.

Rather than being fearful of the end of days, you will discover the following:

---

[1] All scripture from: The Nelson Study Bible. NKJV, copyright 1997 by Thomas Nelson, Inc.

There is no fear in love; but perfect love casts out fear, because fear involves torment. But he who fears has not been made perfect in love.
(1 John 4:17–18)

He who dwells in the secret place of the Most High shall abide under the shadow of the Almighty. I will say of the Lord, "He is my refuge and my fortress; My God, in Him I will trust."
(Psalm 91:1–2)

Any good quest becomes more exciting if someone hands you a treasure map. In *The Groom's Arrival,* the attachment in appendix 3, "The Hebrew Wedding Tradition and the Return of Christ," contains a map of the book's content. Perhaps you will become an explorer as I have been. I invite you: let's explore for God's treasure together!

In the Lord's Service, John A. Cooper

Contents

Preface v
Acknowledgment ix
Chapter 1:   *The First Marriage* 1
Chapter 2:   *Revelation* 5
Chapter 3:   *Choson, the Groom* 11
Chapter 4:   *Kallah, the Bride* 21
Chapter 5:   *Shiddukhin, Selecting a Bride* 25
Chapter 6:   *Mikveh, The Ritual Cleansing* 43
Chapter 7:   *Mohar, The Bride Price* 47
Chapter 8:   *Ketubah, Marriage Covenant* 51
Chapter 9:   *Matan, The Bridal Gift* 63
Chapter 10:   *Eyrusin, The Betrothal* 67
Chapter 11:   *Nisuin, The Presentation* 73
Chapter 12:   *Chuppah, The Bridal Chamber and Ceremony* 79
Chapter 13:   *Yichud, The Seclusion* 105
Chapter 14:   *Seudas Mitzvah, The Marriage Supper* 109
Chapter 15:   *Millennial Reign of Christ* 113
Chapter 16:   *New Heaven and New Earth* 125
Epilogue 131
Final Words 135
Notes 137

appendix 1:   *The Seven Blessings of Revelation*....................141
appendix 2:   *Kingdom History of Israel and Judah*..................143
appendix 3:   *The Hebrew Wedding Tradition and the Return of Christ*....145
appendix 4:   *The Olivet Discourse, Days of Daniel, and Jesus' Scroll*......146
appendix 5:   *Ten Elements of the Hebrew Wedding Tradition*...........147

Acknowledgment

First of all, I wish to praise and glorify the Lord, who gave direction, encouragement, and revelation into His word.

It has been my constant desire to maintain the truth and clarity of the Scripture without, "adding or taking away" (Revelation 22:18–19). I claim no special insight, but I have sought wisdom into these truths through the guidance of the Holy Spirit and prayer.

Many years ago, I was taught the prophetic word through an old-time Evangelical Methodist minister, Reverend Cecil C. Nichols. Pastor Nichols often attended the Winona Lake Conference on Prophecy in northern Indiana. He went home to glory in 2010 at over one hundred years of age.

My training is as an engineer who loves the Word of God. My personal journey with Christ began in November of 1965. Since day one, the discovery of the beauty and mystery of God's Word has been at the center of my love for Him. As a working engineer, I was often assigned projects with completion dates that were as much as two years or more in the future. My passion and desire to complete *The Groom's Arrival* is a process with a similar time frame.

I have attempted to be diligent in biblical scholarship. The *MacArthur Study Bible,* the Nelson *New King James Version* (NKJV*) Study Bible,* and the *English Standard Version* (ESV) *Study Bible* have been my main resources. The Hebrew wedding tradition information is derived from a number of Messianic/Jewish resources. The book *Living Judaism: The Complete Guide to Jewish Belief, Tradition & Practice* by Rabbi Wayne Dosick was especially enlightening when it came to understanding the ancient and current traditions in Judaism.

The text and content of *The Groom's Arrival* have been reviewed with Pastor Chuck Whitmire and Pastor Jeff Davis of Shiloh Christian Union Church. I have taught the material to several groups of peers at the church. The students were helpful in making edits and suggestions for clarity. Shiloh's church secretary, Anita Whitmire, has devoted time and effort to compile and print this book. To all I extend a heartfelt appreciation.

This journey of study began in December of 2008. Little did I know of God's plan of personal hardships to humble and strengthen me during the quest. I am thankful to my wife, Linda, for her constant support, prayers, and patience during my hours of composition at the computer.

Chapter 1

The First Marriage

Tradition

In the Hebrew marriage tradition, the covenant was seen as a commitment before God of the man to his bride. At the betrothal he says, "With this ring you are made holy unto me. There are many other women in the world, but you are like no other." She is permitted no other man; he is permitted no other woman. They are holy, *Qadesh*, sacred and set aside for each other.

In the Old Testament, God's desire is to be "wedded" in a covenant relationship with His chosen people, Israel. The Torah and the Ten Commandments (Exodus 20:1–17) are given as a contract, or *ketubah,* to authenticate Israel's relationship with God. In a sense, the written Law becomes the marriage covenant between God and Israel.

And He (Jesus) answered and said to them, "Have you not read that He who made them at the beginning 'made them male and female, and said, For this reason a man shall leave his father and mother and be joined to his wife, and the two shall become one flesh? So then, they are no longer two but one flesh. Therefore what God has joined together, let not man separate."

(Matthew 19:4–6; referring to Genesis 1:27)

In the beginning God created man. And the LORD *God said, "It is not good that man should be alone; I will make him a helper comparable to him"*

(Genesis 2:18)

> *The woman was created from the rib of man. "And the L*ORD *God caused a deep sleep to fall on Adam, and he slept; and He took one of his ribs, and closed up the flesh in its place. Then the rib which the L*ORD *God had taken from man He made into a woman, and He brought her to the man.*
>
> *And Adam said: "This is now bone of my bones And flesh of my flesh; She shall be called Woman, Because she was taken out of Man." Therefore a man shall leave his father and mother and be joined to his wife, and they shall become one flesh."*
>
> (Genesis 2:21–24)

> *I will betroth you to Me forever; Yes, I will betroth you to Me In righteousness and justice, In loving kindness and mercy; I will betroth you to Me in faithfulness, And you shall know the Lord.*
>
> (Hosea 2:19–20)

The Old Testament Marriage Covenant

Abram is established in his covenant relationship with God *brit* when he declares his belief in one god, *YHWH*. He undergoes *brit milah* (circumcision) as a sign of his new covenant relationship. He is given the new name "Abraham," which means, "Father of a Multitude." God grants him unconditional love, or *chesed* (grace). In effect, God says, "It does not matter if you are perfect, but I am your God and you are my child and I love you with an absolute love." Abraham's faith is counted as righteousness.

There is no more beautiful story of the ancient wedding tradition than that told in the book of Genesis. Father Abraham is desirous of finding a suitable bride for his son Isaac. The bride must be found among his fellow kinsmen, who live far away in Mesopotamia, in the city of Nahor. Abraham sends his most trusted servant to find a bride for Isaac (Genesis chapter 24).

Interwoven in this love story is the remarkable leadership of God. The story also gives insight into an ancient tradition of the Hebrew people. It portrays the importance of how our decisions, even the selection of our mates, are to be guided by God. As you read, it is my hope that you will discover how the tradition speaks to the love of Christ for His Church.

The New Testament Marriage Covenant

The covenant is symbolic of Christ and His desire to be at one with His Church. He comes to earth to seek out His "True Bride." The promises and conditions of the relationship are established through His life and ministry, and they are written down in the pages of the New Testament.

The Old Testament covenant promises were in effect and in place until Christ came. The New Covenant transforms the believers in Christ, making them, the Bride, ready for God's eternal inheritance.

> *For if the blood of bulls and goats and the ashes of a heifer, sprinkling the unclean, sanctifies for the purifying of the flesh, how much more shall the blood of Christ, who through the eternal Spirit offered Himself without spot to God, cleanse your conscience from dead works to serve the living God? And for this reason He is the Mediator of the new covenant, by means of death, for the redemption of the transgressions under the first covenant, that those who are called may receive the promise of the eternal inheritance.*
>
> *(Hebrews 9:13–15)*

Chapter 2

Revelation

Reading Revelation

A. Blessed is he who reads, hears and keeps[2]

Blessed is he who reads and those who hear the words of this prophecy, and keep those things which are written in it; for the time is near.
(Revelation 1:3)

Does the thought of the coming of Jesus frighten you? When you think of His return, do you focus more on thoughts about the tribulation rather than God's plan for our redemption? The "Good News" is that we are not to be afraid of His appearance, because He is coming to claim His Bride, the Church. The Bride is secure in Him.

Question: Why should we read Revelation?

1. We will receive a blessing.
   Revelation 1:3
2. The time is near.
   2 Peter 3:3–4
   1 Thessalonians. 5:1–3
3. It will give us hope in times of despair.
   Titus 2:11–13
4. We will know that our security is in Him.
   1 Corinthians 1:7–8

---

[2] "The Seven Blessings" of Revelation. Complete list is attached in appendix 1.

5. We are told to be ready and watch.
   Matthew 24:36–39
6. Antichrists and false teachers will come.
   Matthew 24:23–25
7. Believers will not suffer God's wrath.
   Romans 5:9

B. *The Revelation of Jesus Christ*

The Revelation of Jesus Christ, which God gave Him to show His servants—things which must shortly take place.
(Revelation 1:1a)

1. The Revelation of Jesus Christ is "unsealed."
   Revelation 22:10
2. Jesus is the author. God instructs Him to reveal it.
   John 8:28–32
3. Jesus Christ becomes clearly visible.
   John 9:35–39

C. The Revelation of Jesus Christ as Revealed through John

And He sent and signified it by His angel to His servant John, who bore witness to the word of God, and to the testimony of Jesus Christ, and to all things that he saw.
(Revelation 1b–2)

1. The Revelation from God, to Christ, to His angel (messenger), to John.
2. John is identified, because he bore witness to the things he saw and because he was faithful to Christ.

D. John Conveys the Message to the Seven Churches

John, to the seven churches which are in Asia: Grace to you and peace from Him who is and was and is to come, and to the seven Spirits who are before His throne, and from Jesus Christ, the faithful witness, the firstborn from the dead, and the ruler over the kings of the earth.
(Revelation 1:4–5a)

1. "Grace and peace."[3]
   1 Corinthians 16:20

---

[3] "Grace" is a NT greeting, and "Peace" is an OT greeting.

2. Stating the eternal nature of God.
   Exodus 33:18–23
   Exodus 34:6–7
3. The seven Spirits of God.
   Isaiah 11:2–3
   Isaiah 61:1–2
4. Identifies Christ, the Author of the letters.
   a. The faithful witness.
      John 8:12–14
   b. The firstborn of the dead
      1 Corinthians 15:20–23
   c. The ruler of the kings of earth
      1 Corinthians 15:24–25

E. Servant Priesthood

To Him who loved us and washed us from our sins in His own blood, and has made us as kings and priests to His God and Father, to Him be glory and dominion forever and ever. Amen.
                                                          (Revelation 1:5b–6)

1. Jesus loves us and has washed us by His own blood.
   1 John 4:17–19
   1 John 1:7
2. Three titles given God's people in the Old Testament (Old Israel).
   A Special Treasure
   A Kingdom of Priests
   A Holy Nation
3. We are called into a servant priesthood with Him.
   John 15: 12–14
   1 John 3:16
   Luke 22:24-27
4. He has made believers to rule and reign with Him (New Israel).
   John 15:16
   Revelation 20:4, 6

Moses is instructed in Exodus chapters 28 and 29 and Leviticus chapter 8 to follow God's design for the priesthood. Through God's instruction, he establishes Aaron and his sons as priests to serve in the earthly temple. There are four stages in the instruction of God. These stages are given to us as a model. All believers are called by Christ into a servant priesthood.

> *And the* LORD *spoke to Moses, saying: "Take Aaron and his sons with him, and the garments, the anointing oil, a bull as the sin offering, two rams, and a basket of unleavened bread; and gather all the congregation together at the door of the tabernacle of meeting. So Moses did as the* LORD *commanded him. And the congregation was gathered together at the door of the tabernacle of meeting. And Moses said to the congregation, "This is what the* LORD *commanded to be done."*
>
> *(Leviticus 8:1–5)*

Question: What are the stages of Servant Priesthood?

Stage #1: Repentance/Conversion/Baptism (cleansed from sin)
  Old Testament (Ritual)
    Exodus 29:4
    Leviticus 8:6
  New Testament (Through Christ)
    Titus 2:14

Stage #2: Transformation/Sanctification (clothed in righteousness)
  Old Testament (Garments)
    Exodus 29:5–6
    Leviticus 8:7–9, 13
    Psalm 132:9, 16
  New Testament
    1 Peter 5:5–6

Stage #3: Anointed for Service (empowered to serve)
  Old Testament
    Exodus 29:7
    Leviticus 8:10–12
  New Testament
    1 John 2:20; 2:27

Stage #4: Atonement and Blood Consecration (set aside for service)
1. Atonement, confession, and the payment for sin
    a. The blood sacrifice of animals (Old Israel).
       Exodus 29:35–37
       Leviticus 1:3–4
       Leviticus 23:26–28
    b. Christ shed blood on behalf of our sins (New Israel).
       Hebrews 9:11–14
       1 John 4:10

2. *There are three instructions* given with Blood Consecration (Leviticus 8:22–24). Priests are "marked" with the blood in three areas: the right earlobe, the right thumb, and the right large toe.
   a. *Listen to God when He speaks* (the right earlobe, ears to hear). Priests are to be still and listen for God to speak.
      Old Testament
         Leviticus 8:33–34
         Psalm 46:10
      New Testament
         Galatians 1:16
      Priests are to speak the Word of God.
      Old Testament
         Leviticus 10:10–11
         Malachi 2:7
      New Testament
         2 Timothy 2:2
         2 Timothy 3:14–17
      Priests are messengers of God to the people.
      Old Testament
         Leviticus 9:5–7
         Leviticus 9:22–24
      New Testament
         Matthew 28:19–20
         2 Corinthians 5:18–20
   b. *Do what God instructs* (the right thumb, hands to serve). Priests are to be obedient to God (i.e., do exactly what God tells you to do).
      Old Testament
         Leviticus 10:1–3
      New Testament
         1 Peter 2:4-5, 9 (i.e., come to Him)
   c. *Go where God sends you* (the right large toe, go to serve). Priests are to "walk" with God.
      Old Testament
         Malachi 2:6
      New Testament
         Galatians 5:16–18, 25

F. *Behold He is coming*

Behold He is coming with clouds, and every eye shall see Him, and they also who pierced Him. And all the tribes of the earth will mourn because of Him. Even so, Amen. "I am the Alpha and the Omega, the Beginning and the End," says the Lord, "who is and who was and is to come, the Almighty."

(Revelation 1:7–8)

1. "He is coming with clouds" (at the end of the tribulation).
   Acts 1:9–11
2. "Every eye will see Him" (every knee will bow).
   Romans 14:10–12
3. "Those who pierced Him."
   Zechariah 12:10–13:1
4. "The tribes of earth will wail" (He brings judgment).
   Matthew 13:36–43
5. "Even so, Amen."
6. "Alpha and Omega."
   The Creator and Finisher
7. "Who was and is to come."
   The one who transcends time and space
   Philippians 2:9-11
8. The Almighty, EL SHADDAI.
   Genesis 17:1

Chapter 3
Choson, the Groom

Choson, The Groom

From the beginning, God knew it was not good for Adam to be alone. So, He made for Adam a helper. Since the woman was taken from the rib of man, Jews consider the man as never being complete without his wife at his side. To a devoted Jew, marriage outside the faith is not to be considered.

The plan to carry out the tradition begins with the father. It dates back to the earliest beginnings of Judaism. The father sees that his son has grown to manhood, and it is time for his marriage. The son has been busy preparing for his life work and tending to his father's property. He has been under the tutelage of his parents and the community elders. His desire is to begin his own family. He receives his father's blessing to begin the process. The groom-to-be is full of hope and dreams.

Just think about it. God's plan has always been to be in a full relationship with us. He is Holy; we are unholy. Yet, His heart is full of love for us. He elects to redeem us with the most revolutionary idea. He will send His Son in the form of a man, fully God and yet fully man. Jesus comes to claim His bride by paying the price for our sinful nature and to make us clean. John the Baptist announces His coming as he proclaims:

> *Behold! The Lamb of God who takes away the sin of the world!*
> *(John 1:29)*

Christ comes seeking His True Bride, God's chosen people, and to establish the Church.

> *The Son of Man has come to seek and to save that which was lost.*
> *(Luke 19:10)*

He begins His ministry by calling the people of Israel into repentance and to the establishment of a New Covenant, one that would be written with His own blood. On Palm Sunday, He is presented at the Holy City of Jerusalem, riding on a donkey.

> *Rejoice greatly, O daughter of Zion! Shout, O daughter of Jerusalem! Behold, your King is coming to you; He is just and having salvation, Lowly and riding on a donkey, A colt, the foal of a donkey.*
> *(Zechariah 9:9)*

Throughout His ministry, He had instructed the disciples to carry God's redemption message to the house of Israel first.

> *These twelve Jesus sent out and commanded them, saying: "Do not go into the way of the Gentiles, and do not enter a city of the Samaritans. But go rather to the lost sheep of the house of Israel."*
> *(Matthew 10:5–6)*

> *He came to His own, and His own did not receive Him.*
> *(John 1:11)*

He comes to Israel as a servant, riding on the back of a donkey as a symbol of peace and humility. But what they wanted was a king—one who conquers and rides on a military horse with his army to free them from the oppressors.

Despite having initially embraced His message, in the end, most in Israel continued to reject Him. In the waning hours of His life on earth, Jesus laments over their rejection:

> *O Jerusalem, Jerusalem, the one who kills the prophets and stones those who are sent to her! How often I wanted to gather your children together, as a hen gathers her chicks under her wings, but you were not willing! See! Your house is left to you desolate; for I say to you, you shall see Me no more till you say,* "Blessed is He who comes in the name of the Lord!"
> (Matthew 23:37–39)

After the events of Holy Week, the disciples are reminded of what He had said earlier. The events marking His crucifixion, death, and resurrection have all occurred as the Groom has sought His True Bride. The betrothal period or "Church Age" begins. The final statements that He made, remind us of the ancient tradition of the Groom's promises to return and claim the Bride. The Revelation of Jesus given to John sets the stage for the Groom's arrival. We await the day when these events will unfold.

> *I go to prepare a place for you, I will come again and receive you to Myself; that where I am, you may be also.*
> (John 14:3)

The Apostle John Encounters the Resurrected Lord

A. John on the Island Patmos[4]

> *I, John, both your brother and companion in tribulation, and in the kingdom and patience of Jesus Christ, was on the island that is called Patmos for the word of God and for the testimony Jesus Christ.*
> (Revelation 1:9)

B. *In the Spirit*

> *I was in the spirit on the Lord's Day, and I heard behind me a loud voice, as of a trumpet.*
> (Revelation 1:10)

John, like Paul in 2 Corinthians, leaves his physical form and is transformed by the Spirit.

---

[4] Revelation was written down in AD 95 or 96, while John was held prisoner on the Roman penal colony on the island of Patmos. The island is approximately 10 x 6 miles in size and off the coast of Asia Minor (Turkey). John's Revelation was with Christ and the messages of things that he had seen, things that are and the things that are to come (Revelation 1:19).

> *I know a man in Christ who fourteen years ago—whether in the body I do not know, or whether out of the body I do not know, God knows—such a one was caught up to the third heaven. And I know such a man—whether in the body or out of the body I do not know, God knows—how he was caught up into Paradise and heard inexpressible words, which it is not lawful for a man to utter.*
>
> (2 Corinthians 12:2–4)

C. Letters to the Seven Churches,[5] Jesus' Proclamation

The glorified Savior announces Himself by proclaiming His heavenly attribute as the Creator and then instructs John to deliver these messages to the Churches:

> *saying, "I am the Alpha and Omega, the First and the Last," and "What you see write in a book and send it to the seven churches which are in Asia: to Ephesus, to Smyrna, to Pergamos, to Thyatira, to Sadis, to Philadelphia, and to Laodicea."*
>
> (Revelation 1:11)

D. *The Voice*

> *Then I turned to see the voice that spoke with me. And having turned I saw seven golden lampstands.*
>
> (Revelation 1:12)

Question: How does He speak to us?

1. He has spoken to us through the prophets.
   1 Samuel 3:1–11
   Ezekiel 2:1–3:15
   Isaiah 6:7–10
   Isaiah 61:1–3
2. Through His Word.
   Romans 10:15–18
   John 6:63
3. Christ speaks His truth to us in a mystery.
   Mark 4:11–12
   1 Corinthians 2: 6–8
   1 Peter 3:12

---

5   The locations are listed in the order of travel.

E. **One like the Son of Man**

John sees the glorified Jesus and uses the symbolic phrase, "*One like the Son of Man.*" Jesus used this phrase often to describe Himself during His ministry.

> *and in the midst of the seven lampstands One like the Son of Man, clothed with a garment down to His feet and girded about the chest with a golden band. His head and His hair were white like wool, and as white as snow, and His eyes like a flame of fire; His feet were like fine brass, as if refined in a furnace, and His voice as the sound of many waters; He had in His right hand seven stars, out of His mouth went a sharp two-edged sword, and His countenance was like the sun shining in its strength.*
>
> (Revelation 1:13–16)

1. "Son of Man," the Messianic title, refers to the mysterious human–divine figure, the one who will be given rule over all the nations.
   Joshua 5:13–15
   Daniel 7:13–14
   John 1:51
2. He acts with authority.
   John 5:26–27
   John 9:39
   Matthew 26:64
3. In Hebrew His name is *Yeshua*, which means, *Ye Hovah is Salvation.*
   Luke 1: 30–33
4. Jesus comes to us in three distinct roles: Prophet, Priest and King
   a. Prophet: Prophets bring the Word of God from God to the people.
      i.   Predicted in Old Testament.
           Deuteronomy 18:15–19
      ii. He preaches the message with authority.
           Matthew 7:28–29
      iii. He is "The Word of Life."
           1 John 1:1–4
           Romans 10:8
   b. Priest: Priests represent the people in coming before God's presence.
      i. The Gospels reveal Christ as priest.
         (Matthew, Mark, Luke, John).
         Hebrews 10:19–22

      ii. Covenant of Law vs. Covenant of Grace.
          Romans 3:21–26
          Romans 5:9–11
      iii. Role of Priest and Sacrifice.
          Hebrews 10:11–14;
          Isaiah 53:10-12
  c. King: The one who brings God's rule to bear on the people.
      i. In His Glory.
         Isaiah 9:6–7
         Revelation 1:7–8
      ii. As King of Righteousness.
          Isaiah 32:1;
          Isaiah 11:1–5
      iii. He comes to judge and make war.
          John 3:18
          John 5:26–27
          John 5:22
          John 12:47–48
          Revelation 19:11
      iv. He comes to abolish death.
          John 8:51
          Romans 8:2, 10, 11
          Romans 6:23
      v. He secures the pure Church as His Bride.
         Matthew 25:1–13
         Revelation 19:6–8
      vi. Order of Melchizedek
          Genesis 14:18–20
          Hebrews 5:5–10
          Hebrews 7:1–3
          Hebrews 7:11–17

F. *I fell at His feet*

And when I saw Him, I [John] fell at His feet as dead. But He laid His right hand on me, saying to me, "Do not be afraid; I am the First and the Last. I am He who lives, and was dead, and behold, I am alive forevermore. Amen. And I have the keys of Hades and of Death".
(Revelation 1:17–18)

Many Old Testament saints experienced the presence and holiness of God. In some instances, these encounters can be interpreted as having been with the Pre-Incarnate Christ. In the New Testament, the Disciples and then Paul encountered the transfigured Jesus.

Examples of Responding to God's Holiness
- Genesis 17:1–5
- Isaiah 6:1–6
- Matthew 17:1–9
- Acts 9:3–6

G. *The things which you have seen*

Write the things which you have seen, and the things which are, and the things which will take place after this. The mystery of the seven stars which you saw in My right hand, and the seven golden lampstands: The seven stars are the angels of the seven churches, and the seven lampstands which you saw are the seven churches.

(Revelation 1:19–20)

The truths that are revealed by Christ in Revelation
1. The person of Jesus and His role in history
2. John's personal experience
3. Things that were in existence at the time
4. Future events
5. Mystery of the stars and lampstands
6. Ministers, messengers, and churches
7. Introduction of the seven churches

H. Christ, the Messianic Bridegroom

1. A descendant of Abraham.
   Matthew 1:1
   Galatians 3:16
2. Of the tribe of Judah.
   Genesis 49:10
   Luke 3:23, 33
3. Eternal and chosen by God.
   Hebrews 1:8–13
4. Born of a virgin.
   Isaiah 7:14
   Matthew 1:18
5. God's Revelation to Joseph.
   Matthew 1:19–21

6. God's Revelation to Simeon.
      Luke 2:25–26
   7. God's Revelation through John the Baptist.
      John 3:28–36

I. Christ, the Word that becomes flesh

   1. God the Father sends Christ's forerunner.
      John 1:6–8
   2. When God speaks, things happen.
      Psalm 33:6–9
      Isaiah 55:11
   3. Christ comes to earth.
      John 1:1; 1:14 (logos)
      Philippians 2:5–7
   4. He comes in the form of a man. Fully man, yet fully God.
      Matthew 1:23
      Mark 1:9–11
   5. He acts in His Father's name and with His Father's authority.
      Matthew 3:17
      Matthew 28:18
   6. The battle for earth begins.
      Matthew 4:1
      Matthew 10:34–39

J. The Lord Is Revealed to the Seven Churches

Revelation Chapters 2 and 3

These are the messages to the Seven Churches given in Revelation chapters 2 and 3. With each letter, Christ introduces Himself with a particular symbolic characteristic that is directed toward each church.

1. Ephesus, *He who holds the seven stars*

> To the angel of the church of Ephesus write, "These things says He who holds the seven stars in His right hand, who walks in the midst of the seven golden lampstands:"
>
> *(Revelation 2:1)*

2. Smyrna, *The First and the Last*

> And to the angel of the church in Smyrna write, "These things says the First and the Last, who was dead, and came to life:"
>
> *(Revelation 2:8)*

3. **Pergamos**, *He who has the sharp two-edged sword*
    And to the angel of the church in Pergamos write, "These things says He who has the sharp two-edged sword:"
    (Revelation 2:12)

4. **Thyatira**, *He who has eyes like a flame and feet like fine brass*
    And to the angel of the church in Thyatira write, "These things says the Son of God, who has eyes like a flame of fire, and His feet like fine brass:"
    (Revelation 2:18)

5. **Sardus**, *He who has the seven Spirits of God*
    And to the angel of the church in Sardis write, "These things says He who has the seven Spirits of God and the seven stars:"
    (Revelation 3:1a)

6. **Philadelphia**, *He who has the key of David*
    And to the angel of the church in Philadelphia write, "These things says He who is holy, He who is true, He who has the key of David, He who opens and no one shuts, and shuts and no one opens:"
    (Revelation 3:7)

7. **Laodicea**, *The Faithful and True Witness*
    And to the angel of the church of the Laodiceans write, "These things says the Amen, the Faithful and True Witness, the Beginning of the creation of God:"
    (Revelation 3:14)

Chapter 4
Kallah, the Bride

Kallah, the Bride

    Kallah is the Hebrew name given for the bride. For devout Jews, it is common for the father of the groom-to-be to select a bride for his son. An example of this is in the Old Testament, when Abraham made arrangements for his son Isaac. Bridal candidates were to be of the Hebrew family and faith.

    It was the bride's father's responsibility to sign the betrothal contract, committing to the condition that he would present his daughter as a "pure virgin" (chaste) at the wedding ceremony.

In Proverbs, we find these two statements:

> *An excellent wife is the crown of her husband. (Proverbs 12:4)*
> *Who can find a virtuous wife? For her worth is far above rubies.*
> *(Proverbs 31:10)*

God's desire has always been to find a Chosen People as His True Bride.

> *"For your Maker is your husband, The LORD of hosts is His name; And your Redeemer is the Holy One of Israel; He is called the God of the whole earth. For the LORD has called you like a woman forsaken and grieved in spirit, Like a youthful wife when you were refused," says your God.*
> *(Isaiah 54:5–6)*

God tells the Hebrews that if they accept His Covenant with them, He will make them "His special treasure."

> *Now therefore, if you will indeed obey My voice and keep My covenant, then you shall be a special treasure to Me above all people; for all the earth is Mine.*
> *(Exodus 19:5)*

The truth is that many times Israel had broken from the requirements of God's covenant and played the part of the harlot.

> *Judah has dealt treacherously, And an abomination has been committed in Israel and in Jerusalem, For Judah has profaned The LORD's holy institution which He loves: He has married the daughter of a foreign god …*
>
> *And this is the second thing you do: You cover the altar of the LORD with tears, With weeping and crying; So He does not regard the offering anymore, Nor receive it with goodwill from your hands. Yet you say, "For what reason?" Because the LORD has been witness between you and the wife of your youth, With whom you have dealt treacherously; Yet she is your companion and your wife by covenant. But did He not make them one, Having a remnant of the Spirit? And why one? He seeks godly offspring. Therefore take heed to your spirit, and let none deal treacherously with the wife of his youth.*
> *(Malachi 2:11, 13–15)*

Sampson went against the Hebrew marriage tradition in Judges chapter 14, when he went to his father and mother to demanded that they, *"get her for me as a wife,"* a woman from Timnah, a Philistine (Judges 14:1–2). The outcome was her betrayal of Sampson to the Philistines. Sampson seeks revenge on the Philistines after they had killed her (Judges 14:6–8).

Despite the rebellion of Israel, God continues to stand fully behind His promises made through the Patriarchs. God continues to pursue those He loves.

> *I will betroth you to Me forever; Yes, I will betroth you to Me in righteousness and justice, In loving kindness and mercy; I will betroth you to Me in faithfulness, And you shall know the* L<small>ORD</small>.
> *(Hosea 2:19–20)*

In the New Testament, Paul clearly states Christ's desire for a continued relationship with a chosen people. In this case, Paul's reference is to the Gentiles in the Church at Corinth.

> *For I am jealous for you with godly jealousy. For I have betrothed you to one husband, that I may present you as a chaste virgin to Christ.*
> *(2 Corinthians 11:2)*

Just like when a man is joined to his wife they are considered as one, when Christ's Bride, the Church, is joined to Christ, it is referred to as "His Body."

> *now rejoice in my sufferings for you, and fill up in my flesh what is lacking in the afflictions of Christ, for the sake of His body, which is the church.*
> *(Colossians 1:24)*

A. The Church as the Bride

1. Christ has first chosen us.
   John 15:16
   2 Thessalonians 2:13–14
2. Christ is building (transforming) us into His Church.
   Ephesians 2:19–22[6]
   1 Peter 2:4–5
3. As the Church, we become His body, made up of many parts.
   Romans 12:4–5
   1 Corinthians 12:27
4. As the Church, we are called the temple of the Holy Spirit.
   1 Corinthians 3:16

---

[6] The cornerstone is the stone from which the builder would line up the rest of the building.

5. As the Church, we are called children of God.
   John 1:12–13
   Romans 8:16–17
6. When we profess Christ, we are the Church.
   Romans 10:8–10

Chapter 5
Shiddukhin, Selecting a Bride

Shiddukhin, Selecting a Bride

Shiddukhin is the first step in the marriage process prior to a legal betrothal. For devout Jews, it is common for the father of the groom to employ a *Shadkhan*, or "matchmaker," in the process of bride selection.

An example of the bride selection process is in the Old Testament, when Abraham made arrangements through his head servant for his son Isaac.

> *Now Abraham was old, well advanced in age; and the* L*ord* *had blessed Abraham in all things. So Abraham said to the oldest servant of his house, who ruled over all that he had, "Please, put your hand under my thigh, and I will make you swear by the* L*ord**, the God of heaven and the God of the earth, that you will not take a wife for my son from the daughters of the Canaanites, among whom I dwell; but you shall go to my country and to my family, and take a wife for my son Isaac."*
>
> *(Genesis 24:1–4)*

Despite God's desire for His people, the repeated actions of Israel in the Old Testament relate to those of an "unfaithful wife."

> *Then the* L*ord* *said to me, "Backsliding Israel has shown herself more righteous than treacherous Judah. Go and proclaim these words toward the north, and say:*
> *'Return, backsliding Israel,' says the* L*ord**; 'I will not cause My anger to fall on you. For I am merciful,' says the* L*ord**; 'I will not remain angry forever. Only acknowledge your iniquity, That you have transgressed against the* L*ord* *your God, And have scattered your charms To alien deities under every green tree, And you have not obeyed My voice,' says the* L*ord**."*
>
> *(Jeremiah 3:11–13)*

The good thing is that God never gives up. He again reaches out to the Hebrew people at the first coming of Christ. He establishes a New Covenant, written in the sacrifice and blood of His own Son. Most of His chosen people refuse His offer. This does not stop God from finding a people to bless. As Gentiles, we are grafted into the Old Testament promises of God, and our names are written in the Lamb's Book of Life. Paul's ministry to the Gentiles is and was a part of God's plan. In a sense, Paul is God's matchmaker for the Gentiles.

A. Jewish and Gentile Believers

The verses of Romans chapter 11 clearly identify that the Bride is made up from the Jewish believers (Messianic Jews) and the Gentile believers. It presupposes that Jewish believers will be in Israel when Christ comes to claim His Bride. Jews who accept Jesus (*Yeshua*) into their lives are a part of God's olive tree and, therefore, will be a part of Christ's Bride.

> *You did not choose Me, but I chose you. (John 15:16a)*

Question: If the sons of Israel are God's chosen, how are Gentile believers accepted?

1. Jesus comes to Israel first.
   Matthew 10:5–6
   Matthew 15:24
2. A remnant of Jews will become believers in Christ.
   Jeremiah 3:14–18
   Romans 11:1–5
3. Gentile believers are included in Christ's search.
   Isaiah 42:1
   Ephesians 3:5–7
   Matthew 28:18–20
4. Believers come by faith.
   Romans 3:29–4:3
5. Gentile believers are "grafted onto" the Hebrew root.
   Romans 11:16–24
   Ephesians 2:11–18

B. Christ Looks for the True Bride in the Church

Revelation chapters 2 and 3, letters to the Churches[7]

The messages to the seven Churches of Revelation are symbolic of what Christ is looking for in the Church, His Bride. Just like the Hebrew patriarchs in the Old Testament, God is sending out His "matchmakers" to find the true Bride for His Son from His people, both Hebrew and Gentile. Each passage represents a part of His search. The search can be interpreted as a picture of the Church's history and at the same time a search from the contemporary Church. The application of the truth contained in each letter is applicable to the churches as a whole, as well as to each of us individually.

Each Church letter has a pattern:
1. **Christ, the one who**[8] …Christ describes Himself to the Church.
2. **What He knows …**
   He uses the phrase, "I know," to address the Churches' spiritual condition.
3. **What He instructs …**
   Words of direction are given to address their spiritual needs.
4. **What He warns …** The consequences of disobedience.
5. **What He promises …** "To the one who overcomes …"

---

7   Note: "Although these were actual historical churches in Asia Minor, they represent the types of churches that have existed throughout the church age. What Christ says to these churches is relevant in all times" (John MacArthur).
8   Covered in chapter 3.

C. Ephesus, the Church that Lost Its First Love

To the angel of the church of Ephesus write, "These things says He who holds the seven stars in His right hand, who walks in the midst of the seven golden lampstands: 'I know your works, your labor, your patience, and that you cannot bear those who are evil. And you have tested those who say they are apostles and are not, and have found them liars; and you have persevered and have patience, and have labored for My name's sake and have not become weary. Nevertheless I have this against you, that you have left your first_love. Remember therefore from where you have fallen; repent and do the first works, or else I will come to you quickly and remove your lampstand from its place—unless you repent. But this you have, that you hate the deeds of the Nicolaitans, which I also hate.'"

He who has an ear, let him hear what the Spirit says to the churches. To him who overcomes I will give to eat from the tree of life, which is in the midst of the Paradise of God.

(Revelation 2:1–7)

Ephesus was the capital city of the Roman province of Asia, located along several major trade routes. It was the site of the statue of the fertility goddess Diana (Acts 19:35), one of the seven wonders of the ancient world.

In Paul's second missionary journey, he teaches at Ephesus for eighteen months (Acts 18:11), after which he returns to Jerusalem (Acts 18:19). On Paul's third journey, he returns to Ephesus in AD 53 (Acts 19:1), where he begins two more years of ministry. He meets a great opposition from Jews and those who worship Diana (Acts 19:9–10). After Paul's departure, Timothy pastors at the Church for another year and a half (1 Timothy 1:3–4), during which time the Church continues to struggle with those who bring in false doctrine.

John's writing in Revelation occurs nearly thirty years later and continues to caution the Church at Ephesus to be on guard against those who teach false doctrine. They had forgotten the fire and passion of the Holy Spirit as the Gospel was first introduced to them in Acts 19:1–6. It is a warning to us to keep our passion for the Lord at a "first love" level.

    2. **What He knows … (Verses 2:2–3, 6)**
        a. Their works and patient endurance.
           Hebrews 6:10–12
        b. Guard against false teaching.
           Acts 6:5 (Nicolaitans[9])
           Revelation 2:14–15
           Acts 19:26–28 (Diana worship, i.e., civic, economic, and religious)

---

9   Some connect Nicolas, who was a member of the Church in Jerusalem, with starting this false teaching. It may contain elements of Jewish tradition that are counter to NT teachings.

3. **What He instructs … (Verses 2:4–5)**
    a. *Repent* and return to your earlier works.
       Acts 20:28-30
    b. *Remember* where you've been and what Christ has done.
       i. Paul's ministry of more than three years.
          Acts 20:31–32
       ii. Paul's instructions to the Church at Ephesus.
           Ephesians 1:1–2
    c. *Rediscover* your First Love.
       i. Love the Lord above all.
          Matthew 22:37–38
       ii. Love God by following His commandments.
           Matthew 5:16–20
       iii. OT Hebrew confession.[10]
            Deuteronomy 6:4–5
       iv. The OT practice of *Shema*
           Deuteronomy 6:6–9
       v. True love or lip service?
          Matthew 23:1–12
       vi. The blessings of loving the Lord.
           Deuteronomy 11:13–19

4. **What He warns … (Verse 2:5)**
    a. Repent, or He will remove the Church.
       Deuteronomy 11:26–28, 32

5. **What He promises … (Verse 2:7)**
    a. He will grant the right to the "Tree of Life."
       Revelation 22:2, 14

D. Smyrna, the Church under Persecution

And to the angel of the church in Smyrna write, "These things says the First and the Last, who was dead, and came to life: 'I know your works, tribulation, and poverty (but you are rich); and I know the blasphemy of those who say they are Jews and are not, but are a synagogue of Satan. Do not fear any of those things which you are about to suffer. Indeed, the devil is about to throw some of you into prison, that you may be tested, and you will have tribulation ten days. Be faithful until death, and I will give you the crown of life.'"

---

10   The Hebrew tradition uses a special recitation to express their love to God called "*Shema*".

He who has an ear, let him hear what the Spirit says to the churches. He who overcomes shall not be hurt by the second death.
(Revelation 2:8–11)

Smyrna was a Roman harbor known for temples and public buildings dedicated to Roman emperors. Later, Jewish opposition to Christians brought about the martyrdom of Polycarp and Pionius in the second and third centuries.

2. **What He knows … (Verses 2:9–10)**
   a. **Tribulation/Persecution**
      i. The enemies of our souls.
         Psalm 143:3–5
      ii. Christ was persecuted/we will be persecuted.
         John 15:18–21
      iii. Paul persecuted the early Church.
         Acts 22:1–8
      iv. Special blessing for the persecuted.
         Matthew 5:10–12
      v. Holding steady under persecution.
         2 Corinthians 4:8–11
      vi. How to respond to those who persecute.
         Matthew 5:43–47
      vii. Jews of that day persecute the Church.
         1 Thessalonians 2:14–16
      viii. Children of Hagar persecute the Church.
         Galatians 4:23–31
      ix. Satan persecutes the Church.
         Revelation 12:13
   b. **Poverty**
      i. Christ became poor for our sake.
         2 Corinthians 8:9
      ii. Special Invitation for the poor.
         Luke 14:13–14
      iii. Special blessings for the poor.
         Luke 6:20–23
      iv. A place of honor for the poor.
         James 2:2–5
      v. Help for the poor.
         Luke 18:22

       vi. Abundance of the heart.
       Luke 21:2–4
       vii. Hear the cry of the poor.
       Proverbs 21:13
   c. **Suffering**
       i. Jesus suffered for us.
       Luke 24:46–48
       ii. Being counted worthy when you suffer.
       Acts 5:40–41
       Philippians 1:27–30
       2 Timothy 3:10–12
       iii. Suffering brings growth.[11]
       2 Corinthians 12:7–10
       iv. Upholding each other during suffering.
       1 Corinthians 12:26–27
       v. Being content while suffering.
       Philippians 4:12–13
       vi. God reveals Himself in suffering.
       Romans 8:18–22
       vii. Suffering for doing good.
       1 Peter 3:13–17
       viii. Suffering for giving testimony.
       2 Timothy 1:8–12

3. **What He instructs … (Verse 2:10)**
   a. Do not fear while under trial/test.
      John 16:1–4, 33

4. **What He warns … (Verse 2:10)**
   a. Those who fail will face the second death.
      Revelation 20:14–15
      Revelation 21:8

5. **What He promises … (Verse 2:10–11)**
   a. Be faithful and receive the "Crown of Life."
      1 Corinthians 9:24–25
   b. They will not be hurt by the second death.
      Revelation 20:6

---

11 In general, our culture seeks to avoid this kind of growth, whereas great growth occurs in parts of the world during a time of persecution and suffering.

E. Pergamos, the Church that Compromises

And to the angel of the church in Pergamos write,
"These things says He who has the sharp two-edged sword: 'I know your works, and where you dwell, where Satan's throne is. And you hold fast to My name, and did not deny My faith even in the days in which Antipas was My faithful martyr, who was killed among you, where Satan dwells. But I have a few things against you, because you have there those who hold the doctrine of Balaam, who taught Balak to put a stumbling block before the children of Israel, to eat things sacrificed to idols, and to commit sexual immorality. Thus you also have those who hold the doctrine of the Nicolaitans, which thing I hate. Repent, or else I will come to you quickly and will fight against them with the sword of My mouth.'"

He who has an ear, let him hear what the Spirit says to the churches. To him who overcomes I will give some of the hidden manna to eat. And I will give him a white stone, and on the stone a new name written which no one knows except him who receives it.

(Revelation 2:12–2:17)

Pergamos was an important center for pagan and imperial religion. The Church faced both persecutions and dangerous religious deception. Pergamos had built a temple to Caesar in 29 BC and was a center of Caesar worship. The temples to Emperor Augustus, Asklepios (snakelike god of healing), and Zeus were in Pergamos.

2. **What He knows … (Verses 2:13–15)**
   a. Your (good) works.
      i. Hold fast (confess) to His name.
         Matthew 10:32–33
      ii. Antipas and Stephen, witnesses martyred.
         Acts 7:59–60
   b. Dwell in a place of evil.
      i. Oppressive Paganism.
         1 Corinthians 10:19–23
   c. Some are not holding to the faith.
      i. Influence of false teaching.
         Numbers 22–24[12]
         2 Peter 2:12–16

---

12 The teaching of Balaam (adultery/greed) practiced. In Numbers 22–24 Balak, king of the Moabites, persuaded the prophet Balaam by paying him money to go and prophesy against the children of Israel. Even though Balaam knew that it was against God's will, he finally agreed to go. On the way, he was stopped by the Angel of the Lord, who spoke to him through a donkey.

       ii. Using things sacrificed to idols.
           Acts 15:28–29
      iii. Sexual immorality.
           1 Corinthians 6:12–17
      iv. Teaching of the Nicolaitans.[13]
           Acts 6:5
           Revelation 2:6

3. **What He instructs ... (Verse 2:16)** Repent from ...
   a. Being double-minded.
      Matthew 6:24
      James 1:5–8
   b. Sexually immorality.
      1 Corinthians 6:18–20
   c. Root out false teaching.
      1 Timothy 4:1–3

4. **What He warns ... (Verse 2:16)** Consequence of failure ...
   a. Christ will come to bring judgment.
      Psalm 95:7–11

5. **What He promises ... (Verse 2:17)**
   a. To the one who conquers.
      Romans 8:37–39
   b. Hidden manna (soul food).
      Psalm 78:23–25
      Matthew 4:4
   c. White stone.[14]
      1 Peter 2:4–5
   d. With a new name.[15]
      Isaiah 62:2–5
   e. He will reveal hidden mysteries.
      Matthew 13:11–17
      Colossians 1:24–27

F. Thyatira, the Church that Has Become Corrupt

And to the angel of the church in Thyatira write, "These things says the Son of God, who has eyes like a flame of fire, and His feet like fine brass: 'I know your works, love, service, faith, and your patience; and

---

13 See footnote⁹ for Revelation 2:6.
14 A victor's stone was given to the winner in a contest.
15 A new name was given as a symbol of a new status.

as for your works, the last are more than the first. Nevertheless I have a few things against you, because you allow that woman Jezebel, who calls herself a prophetess, to teach and seduce My servants to commit sexual immorality and eat things sacrificed to idols. And I gave her time to repent of her sexual immorality, and she did not repent. Indeed I will cast her into a sickbed, and those who commit adultery with her into great tribulation, unless they repent of their deeds. I will kill her children with death, and all the churches shall know that I am He who searches the minds and hearts. And I will give to each one of you according to your works.'"

Now to you I say, and to the rest in Thyatira, as many as do not have this doctrine, who have not known the depths of Satan, as they say, I will put on you no other burden. But hold fast what you have till I come. And he who overcomes, and keeps My works until the end, to him I will give power over the nations—

"He shall rule them with a rod of iron;
They shall be dashed to pieces like the potter's vessels--"
as I also have received from My Father; and I will give him the morning star.

He who has an ear, let him hear what the Spirit says to the churches.
(Revelation 2:18–29)

Thyatira had been in Roman hands for more than two centuries before Christ. It was located in a geographical location weak to defend against Rome's enemies and, therefore, was used mainly as an outpost garrison. Corruption comes from weakness. Weakness to attack was the mark of Thyatira.

2. What He knows ... (Verse 2:19)
    a. Your love.
        Romans 13:8–10
        James 2:8–10
    b. Your faith as evidenced by your works.
        James 2:18
    c. Your patience.
        James 1:2–4

3. What He instructs ... (Verses 2:20–21)
    a. Be cautious about spiritual seduction.[16]
        2 Corinthians 11:13–15

---

16   Beguilement: reaching a wrong conclusion by false reasoning. Satan is the master at giving false advice.

      b. Lack of discernment[17] (not able to hear, perceive, and follow the truth).
         2 Corinthians 11:3–4
      c. Sexual immorality and idol worship (moral lapses).
         Galatians 5:16–21
      d. Seared conscience (incapable of clear spiritual and moral thinking).
         Romans 2:14–16
         Titus 1:15–16

4. **What He warns … (Verses 2:22–25)**
    a. Repent from following false teaching and heresy.
       2 Peter 2:1–3
    b. He will search their hearts and minds (consciences).
       1 Peter 3:15–16
       1 John 3:18–21
    c. He will judge their works to see if they are true (avoid divisiveness).
       1 Corinthians 3:11–15
    d. Hold fast to sound teaching and doctrine.
       2 Timothy 3:14–17

5. **What He promises … (Verses 2:26–29)**
    a. To he who overcomes (courageous men of valor).
       1 John 5:4–5
    b. Authority to rule with Him (starting with apostles).
       Matthew 19:27–30
       1 Corinthians 6:1–3
    c. Given a morning star (having His Word in its fullness).
       2Peter 1:17-21

G. Sardus, the Church with no Spiritual Life

And to the angel of the church in Sardis write,

"These things says He who has the seven Spirits of God and the seven stars: 'I know your works, that you have a name that you are alive, but you are dead. Be watchful, and strengthen the things which remain, that are ready to die, for I have not found your works perfect before God. Remember therefore how you have received and heard; hold fast and repent. Therefore if you will not watch, I will come upon you as a thief,

---

17 Satan uses lies that seem to be the truth. Not all religious people are children of God, only those who have believed in Jesus and follow Him.

and you will not know what hour I will come upon you. You have a few names even in Sardis who have not defiled their garments; and they shall walk with Me in white, for they are worthy. He who overcomes shall be clothed in white garments, and I will not blot out his name from the Book of Life; but I will confess his name before My Father and before His angels."'

He who has an ear, let him hear what the Spirit says to the churches.
(Revelation 3:1–6)

Sardus was the home of Aesop (Aesop's fables). It was noted for its wool production and its vineyards for making wine. Several times in its history, outsiders attacked Sardus. As the story goes, the watchmen who were to warn of the attack were sound asleep, maybe from too much wine. Like Sardus, constant vigilance by the Church is needed for survival.

2. **What He knows … (Verse 3:1b, 3:4a)**
    a. Your imperfect works.
       Ephesians 2:1–3;
       Ephesians 2:10
    b. Even so, there are some who are worthy.
       Colossians 1:10

3. **What He instructs … (Verse 3:2)**
    a. Be watchful.
       2 Timothy 4:2–5
    b. Bring to life that which is nearly dead.
       Romans 6:11–14

4. **What He warns … (Verse 3:3)**
    a. Remember, and, "Wake up!"
       Romans 13:11–14
    b. Repent, and, "Hold fast."
       1 Corinthians 15:1–2;
    c. Watchmen are to be alert.
       Ezekiel 3:17–21

5. **What He promises … (Verse 3:4b, 3:5)**
    a. He will walk with them.
       Psalm 23:1–4
    b. He who overcomes will be clothed in white.
       Isaiah 1:18

    c. Names will not be "blotted out."[18]
        Revelation 20:12, 15, 21:27
        Exodus 32:30-35
    d. He will confess them before the Father.
        Matthew 10:32

H. Philadelphia, the Faithful Church

And to the angel of the church in Philadelphia write,
"These things says He who is holy, He who is true, 'He who has the key of David, He who opens and no one shuts, and shuts and no one opens.' I know your works. See, I have set before you an open door, and no one can shut it; for you have a little strength, have kept My word, and have not denied My name. Indeed I will make those of the synagogue of Satan, who say they are Jews and are not, but lie—indeed I will make them come and worship before your feet, and to know that I have loved you. Because you have kept My command to persevere, I also will keep you from the hour of trial which shall come upon the whole world, to test those who dwell on the earth. Behold, I am coming quickly! Hold fast what you have, that no one may take your crown. He who overcomes, I will make him a pillar in the temple of My God, and he shall go out no more. I will write on him the name of My God and the name of the city of My God, the New Jerusalem, which comes down out of heaven from My God. And I will write on him My new name."
He who has an ear, let him hear what the Spirit says to the churches.
(Revelation 3:7–13)

The word "Philadelphia" comes from the Greek and means "brotherly love." The name comes from the founder who, three centuries earlier, was noted for his unusual devotion to his brother. The Church was being persecuted by the local Jews. Despite being low in number and having little strength, the believers had been faithful to Christ.

In the Old and New Testaments, the Jews looked down on the Gentiles. At the time this was written, the local synagogue was serving the purposes of Satan. In the future, the persecutors will be humbled before God for their actions.

At the end of the age, a time of testing falls upon all the earth. The question surrounding the verse in Revelation 3:10 is whether it shows removal (Pre-tribulation, Rapture) of the believers at the start of the Tribulation or protection

---

18   City officials would "blot out" the names of undesirables from the city roll and deny them access .

through the trial. Pre-tribulationalists base their reasoning on the Greek form of the words "to keep" followed by the words "from" or "out of."

"The Tribulation" refers to the seven-year period of God's judgments being released upon the rebellious world and detailed throughout Revelation chapters 6 through 19. The latter half is referred to as "The Great Tribulation."

2. **What He knows ... (Verse 3:8–9)**
    a. Open door, opportunity for ministry (vs. the closed door of Revelation 3:20).
       1 Corinthians 16:9
       Colossians 4:2–6
    b. Open door, access to heaven.
       Revelation 4:1
    c. Your strength under trial.
       2 Corinthians 12:9–10
       1 Peter 4:12–14
    d. The Jews who reject you will be humbled by your love.
       Matthew 5:44
       Romans 12:17–21

3. **What He instructs ... (Verse 3:10–11)**
    a. Persevere.
       2 Peter 2:7–9
    b. "Hold fast"[19] to the crown of life.
       Hebrews 4:14–15

4. **What He warns ... (Verse 3:11)**
    a. I will come quickly.[20]
       1 Corinthians 16:22
       1 Thessalonians 5:3-4
       Revelation 22:20

5. **What He promises ... (Verse 3:10–12)**
    a. The trial (tribulation) is for those in rebellion against God.
       Isaiah 26:20–27:1
    b. "Hold fast," and He will give you the victor's crown.[21]
       1 Corinthians 9:24-25
    c. He will make you a pillar in the House of God.[22]
       Jeremiah 1:18–19

---

19 "Crown" is not a referral to a king's crown but to a wreath worn by a winning athlete.
20 NT churches use the Aramaic word *Maranatha*.
21 Those who suffer martyrdom will be transformed and made triumphant.
22 The victor can never be excluded from God's presence.

I. Laodicea, the Lukewarm Church

And to the angel of the church of the Laodiceans write,

"These things says the Amen, the Faithful and True Witness, the Beginning of the creation of God: 'I know your works, that you are neither cold nor hot. I could wish you were cold or hot. So then, because you are lukewarm, and neither cold nor hot, I will vomit you out of My mouth. Because you say, 'I am rich, have become wealthy, and have need of nothing'—and do not know that you are wretched, miserable, poor, blind, and naked—I counsel you to buy from Me gold refined in the fire, that you may be rich; and white garments, that you may be clothed, that the shame of your nakedness may not be revealed; and anoint your eyes with eye salve, that you may see. As many as I love, I rebuke and chasten. Therefore be zealous and repent. Behold, I stand at the door and knock. If anyone hears My voice and opens the door, I will come in to him and dine with him, and he with Me. To him who overcomes I will grant to sit with Me on My throne, as I also overcame and sat down with My Father on His throne.'"

He who has an ear, let him hear what the Spirit says to the churches.

(Revelation 3:14–22)

Laodicea was one of the most wealthy and prosperous cities of the era. It was surrounded by an extensive wall and had two theaters and a Roman stadium. It was noted for its banking, wool, and medicines (eye salve). In AD 60, it was damaged by an earthquake, but it refused help from the Roman government and did its own rebuilding.

Laodicea had an inadequate water supply, so an underground aqueduct was constructed. The water was of questionable quality (maybe surface water), unlike the clear cold springs that supplied other cities. Some ancient cities also had hot springs, which were useful for bathing and healing. Laodicea had neither, so the phrase, "You are lukewarm," fits its description.

In Paul's writing to the Church in Colossae, he specifically mentions both those at Laodicea and Colossae as being in conflict with the Gospel. There appears to have been a strong Jewish presence in the city. Colossians 2:4–10 points toward their dependence on "persuasive words," "philosophy," and the "traditions of men" in living out their faith. Paul points out these faults to steer them away from their superior attitudes and to help bring them to humility and maturity. John's writing almost thirty years later in Revelation suggests their ongoing struggle.

> *But if ye will not do so, behold, ye have sinned against the LORD: and be sure your sin will find you out.*
>
> *(Numbers 32:23 KJV)*

2. **What He knows ... (Verse 3:15–17)**
   a. Your works.
      Colossians 2:1–10
   b. Neither hot or cold (character defects/intellectual superiority).
      Matthew 7:21–23
      Matthew 7:24–27
   c. Your boasting (self-delusion).
      Proverbs 16:18–19
      1 John 2:15-16
   d. Your riches (self-reliance and pride).
      Psalm 52:7
      1 Timothy 6:17

3. **What He instructs ... (Verse 3:18)**
   a. Buy gold from Christ (wisdom).
      Job 28:20–28
      Proverbs 1:1–7
   b. Buy white garments (being covered by Christ's righteousness).
      i. Wash first and be clean.
         Isaiah 1:16–18
      ii. White garments for Christ.
         Matthew 17:1–2
         Mark 9:2–3
      iii. White garments for holy angels.
         Matthew 28:2–3
         Mark 16:5
      iv. White garments for those in the Glorified Church.
         Revelation 19:8, 14
   c. Anoint your eyes (to see Jesus who is before you).
      Matthew 13:14–17

4. **What He warns ... (Verse 3:19–20)**
   a. Repent.
      Acts 17:26–31
   b. He will rebuke and chasten.[23]
      Proverbs 15:31–33
      Hebrews 12:5–8

---

23 There are three levels of God's discipline: rebuking, chastening, scourging.

c. Doors of opportunity.[24]
   Luke 12:35–40

5. What He promises … (Verses 3:20–21)
   a. To sit with Him in heavenly places.
      Luke 19:15–19

---

24 Unlike the open door to Philadelphia, Laodicea faces a closed door, which they must open in order to fellowship with Christ, who stands outside.

Chapter 6
Mikveh, The Ritual Cleansing

Mikveh, the Ritual Cleansing

The Hebrew word *mikvah* means "pool" or, more specifically, "living water." After the selection of the bridal candidate, the next step of the betrothal process would be taken. The word *kinddushin* means "sanctification" or "set apart." Prior to the meeting, both the bride and groom would undergo a separate ritual cleansing called a *mikvah*.

Mikvah / baptism is rooted in the Old Testament cleansing in preparation for service before God or when one entered the temple grounds in Jerusalem. At the door of the tabernacle, believers were first "cleansed" with water (stage one) and then "clothed" (stage two) in their ritual garments.

In the New Testament, it is the first step toward the "servant priesthood" of all believers (see the discussion in chapter 2).

After the *mikvah*, the groom and his witnesses would proceed to the bride's home and meet with the bride's father.

A. Purification and Baptism

At the time of Jesus, there were a number of cleansing pools available in Jerusalem. More than likely, there would have been a charge to the public for using the *mikvah* prior to their entry into the holy sites. The rich would have the means to participate, whereas the poor would be left out. John's baptism was done in contrast to the ritualism of the Scribes and Pharisees. The poor would have more openly responded to John's invitation for spiritual cleansing and repentance.

For the Church, the act of Baptism began with John the Baptist and continues today. True baptism is a part of the Christian church ritual as a public sign of our redemption. It should never be raised to the level of a substitute for the new birth in Christ, but it should be a step of public confession and identification with the church. It is the starting point of a life dedicated in service to Him. In the church, we are baptized into Christ's death and resurrection. Second, we are symbolically "baptized" (consecrated) by the Lord with the gift of the Holy Spirit as we receive Christ into our lives.

Question: Why should believers be baptized?

> *Jesus answered, "Most assuredly, I say to you, unless one is born of water and the Spirit, he cannot enter the kingdom of God. That which is born of the flesh is flesh, and that which is born of the Spirit is spirit."*
> *(John 3:5–6)*

1. Symbol of the Old Testament purification.
   Exodus 40:12–13
   Exodus 40:30–32
   Ephesians 5:25–27
2. Symbolic of Christ's death and resurrection.
   Romans 6:3–5
3. Symbolic of the giving of the Holy Spirit.
   Exodus 40:14–15
   John 7: 37–39
4. Figurative of Noah's "ark" of safety by faith in Christ.
   1 Peter 3:20–22
5. Jesus' Baptism and John's testimony.
   Matthew 3:13–17
   Luke 3:16
   John 1:31–34
6. Baptism and Repentance.
   Acts 2:38
   Acts 19:1–9

B. Conversion Practice in Ancient Judaism

When a non-Jew wanted to convert to Judaism, there are certain steps to be taken. Most of us know that male converts would undergo *brit milah*, or ritual circumcision. There is another step that is less familiar. Male and female converts were to be immersed at a ritual cleansing, *mikvah*, where the proselyte is said to be "reborn." Following the ritual, the convert was brought before a rabbinic court, called *beit din*, where the convert is questioned by a team of three rabbis regarding his or her knowledge and commitment to Judaism. At the conversion ceremony, the converts were given a new Jewish name and officially accepted into the Jewish community.

Chapter 7
Mohar, The Bride Price

Mohar, the Bride Price

Two thousand years ago, it was the custom of most cultures to buy and sell brides. Women had no property or inheritance rights. Judaism was the first culture to create a written document, the *ketubah*, or marriage contract, that protects the rights of women. The wife would maintain the sole copy of the document as her guarantee. The Hebrews were the first to practice a means of protecting the status of women as they entered marriage.

When the groom arrives at the bride's parents' house, he brings with him the *ketubah*. It is presented to the bride-to-be and her father.

The *mohar*, or "bride price," is what the groom is willing to pay the father for permission to marry his daughter. In Judaism, it was usual for much of the value of the *mohar* to be added to the bride's personal possessions.

A Bride for Isaac

> *Then Laban and Bethuel answered and said, "The thing comes from the LORD; we cannot speak to you either bad or good. Here is Rebekah before you; take her and go, and let her be your master's son's wife, as the LORD has spoken."*
>
> *And it came to pass, when Abraham's servant heard their words, that he worshiped the LORD, bowing himself to the earth. Then the servant brought out jewelry of silver, jewelry of gold, and clothing, and gave them to Rebekah. He also gave precious things to her brother and to her mother.*
>
> *(Genesis 24:50–53)*

A Bride for Jacob

> *So Jacob served seven years for Rachel, and they seemed only a few days to him because of the love he had for her.*
>
> *And Laban said, "It must not be done so in our country, to give the younger before the firstborn. Fulfill her week, and we will give you this one also for the service which you will serve with me still another seven years."*
>
> *Then Jacob did so and fulfilled her week. So he gave him his daughter Rachel as wife also.*
>
> *(Genesis 29:20, 26–28)*

Jesus' presentation as the Groom and the righteous Davidic Messiah before Israel was on Palm Sunday, when He rode into Jerusalem. Even at the beginning of Christ's presentation before Israel, most begin to reject Him.

> *Rejoice greatly, O daughter of Zion! Shout, O daughter of Jerusalem! Behold, your King is coming to you; He is just and having salvation, Lowly and riding on a donkey, A colt, the foal of a donkey.*
>
> *(Zechariah 9:9)*

For the Church, the bride dowry was paid when Christ offered up Himself for our sins. Unlike Moses' and the repetitive animal sacrifices through the priesthood of Aaron, Christ's "blood sacrifice" was paid once and for all. He sanctifies those who believe on His name. We do not have to pay the price, He already has!

> *The next day John saw Jesus coming toward him, and said, "Behold! The Lamb of God who takes away the sin of the world!"*
>
> *(John 1:29)*

A. Blood Covenants

1. The agreement between God and Man.
   Old Testament: Exodus 12:12–14
   New Testament: 1 Peter 1:18–19
2. The shedding of blood and righteousness.
   Old Testament: Leviticus 17:11
   New Testament: Matthew 26:28
3. Conditions in the Law and justification.
   Old Testament: Hebrews 9:18–20
   New Testament: Romans 3:20–26

B. Christ pays the price

1. The rejected suitor.
   Old Testament:: Isaiah 53:1,3
   New Testament: Luke 18:31-33
2. His sacrifice precedes our acceptance.
   Old Testament: Isaiah 53:5
   New Testament: Romans 5:8
3. He willingly took our guilt and punishment on Himself.
   Old Testament: Isaiah 53:7
   New Testament: 1 Peter 2:21-24
4. He pays the price.
   Old Testament: Isaiah 53:6, 8
   New Testament: 2 Corinthians 5:21
5. By His sacrifice, many are justified.
   Old Testament: Isaiah 53:10-12
   New Testament: Romans 5:15-18

Chapter 8
Ketubah, Marriage Covenant

> ### *Ketubah, the Marriage Covenant*
>
> The word *ketubah* means written. It includes the conditions of the contract and the promises made by the groom to the bride and her family. The groom stipulates the contents of the bride's dowry and pledges to support his wife-to-be. In looking for his bride, the groom is looking for the inner beauty that comes through the application of a God-centered lifestyle.
>
> Even though Rebekah's marriage to Issac was arranged, it appears that she had the right of consent (Genesis 24:5). If the parties come to an agreement, the contract would be signed and the signing confirmed by the groomsmen. The groom would then offer the bride and her father the "Cup of Acceptance." This cup of wine represents the act of sealing the blood covenant. When the bride and her father drink the wine, it signals their acceptance. It is a "blood covenant promise" which is the highest form of commitment in Judaism. The signing and cup exchange were held under the temporary bridal canopy, or *chuppah*.
>
> The bride willingly prepares herself to become the groom's wife by following the principles (beatitudes) that will define their marriage. The physical intimacy in the marriage will not occur at this time, but only at the time of the *yichud*, during the wedding supper and *chuppah*. The union agreement would be in full effect from this point forward and could only be broken by a severe violation of the contract and only by a decree of divorce.
>
> She knows that the groom-to-be will soon depart to prepare his father's home for their life together, but he leaves her with the promises of the marriage covenant, which will bring her hope and joy as she looks forward to the day of his return.

After the great flood and His covenant with Noah, God continues to seek a people to bless. He finds the man Abram to be a man of faith who God claims as righteous. He then makes a sevenfold covenant with Abraham and makes his descendants a chosen people.

> Now the LORD had said to Abram: "Get out of your country, From your family And from your father's house, To a land that I will show you. I will make you a great nation; I will bless you and make your name great; And you shall be a blessing I will bless those who bless you, And I will curse him who curses you; And in you all the families of the earth shall be blessed."
>
> *(Genesis 12:1–3)*

Ketubah, the Marriage Covenant

The Torah, the first five books of the Old Testament, represent God's *ketubah*, or marriage covenant, with His people Israel. God gives the Ten Commandments to Moses. The first term in the covenant contract stipulates Israel's commitment to fidelity in the marriage:

> *I am the LORD your God, who brought you out of the land of Egypt, out of the house of bondage. "You shall have no other gods before Me."*
>
> *(Exodus 20:2–3)*

In recent times, the Jewish people drink four cups of wine with the Passover meal to affirm the covenant made by God in Exodus 6. The four cups represent the four promises of God to Israel. The final cup of wine symbolizes Israel's acceptance of God's terms in their covenant relationship with Him. In the four promises of the covenant God says, "I will."

> *Therefore say to the children of Israel: "I am the LORD; I will bring you out from under the burdens of the Egyptians, I will rescue you from their bondage, and I will redeem you with an outstretched arm and with great judgments. I will take you as My people, and I will be your God. Then you shall know that I am the LORD your God who brings you out from under the burdens of the Egyptians."*
>
> *(Exodus 6:6–7)*

The *ketubah* is a symbolic illustration of the relationship that a believer receives when he puts his trust in Christ as Savior. God's New Covenant promises begin with Jesus. Jesus' first message to the children of Israel is a simple one:

> *"Repent, for the kingdom of heaven is at hand."*
>
> *(Matthew 4:17)*

The children of Israel hear the words of Christ, but most continue to reject God's attempt to make them His chosen people. The meaning hidden in Jesus' parable of the Wicked Vinedresser in Matthew chapter 21 clarifies the position that Israel places itself by rejecting His authority.

Hear another parable: There was a certain landowner who planted a vineyard and set a hedge around it, dug a winepress in it and built a tower. And he leased it to vinedressers and went into a far country. Now when vintage-time drew near, he sent his servants to the vinedressers, that they might receive its fruit. And the vinedressers took his servants, beat one, killed one, and stoned another. Again he sent other servants, more than the first, and they did likewise to them. Then last of all he sent his son to them, saying, "They will respect my son." But when the vinedressers saw the son, they said among themselves, "This is the heir. Come, let us kill him and seize his inheritance." So they took him and cast him out of the vineyard and killed him.

Therefore, when the owner of the vineyard comes, what will he do to those vinedressers?

They said to Him, "He will destroy those wicked men miserably, and lease his vineyard to other vinedressers who will render to him the fruits in their seasons."

Jesus said to them, "Have you never read in the Scriptures: 'The stone which the builders rejected has become the chief cornerstone? This was the LORD's *doing, And it is marvelous in our eyes'?*

"Therefore I say to you, the kingdom of God will be taken from you and given to a nation bearing the fruits of it. And whoever falls on this stone will be broken; but on whomever it falls, it will grind him to powder."

(Matthew 21:33–44)

For three years, Jesus roams the hills of Judea and gathers a following of disciples. He teaches and proclaims the coming of God's kingdom. Through His own blood and sacrifice, the bride price will be paid. Near the end of His time on earth, He meets with the closest circle of His followers and asks a most profound question:

He asked His disciples, saying, "Who do men say that I, the Son of Man, am?"

So they said, "Some say John the Baptist, some Elijah, and others Jeremiah or one of the prophets."

He said to them, "But who do you say that I am?"

> *Simon Peter answered and said, "You are the Christ, the Son of the living God."*
>
> *Jesus answered and said to him, "Blessed are you, Simon Bar-Jonah, for flesh and blood has not revealed this to you, but My Father who is in heaven. And I also say to you that you are Peter, and on this rock I will build My church, and the gates of Hades shall not prevail against it. And I will give you the keys of the kingdom of heaven, and whatever you bind on earth will be bound in heaven, and whatever you loose on earth will be loosed in heaven."*
>
> *Then He commanded His disciples that they should tell no one that He was Jesus the Christ.*
>
> *(Matthew 16:13b–20)*

Just like with the Cup of Acceptance, Jesus seals the New Covenant by drinking the cup of wine at the last supper. The New Covenant is a blood covenant promise.

> *And as they were eating, Jesus took bread, blessed and broke it, and gave it to the disciples and said, "Take, eat; this is My body."*
>
> *Then He took the cup, and gave thanks, and gave it to them, saying, "Drink from it, all of you. For this is My blood of the new covenant, which is shed for many for the remission of sins. But I say to you, I will not drink of this fruit of the vine from now on until that day when I drink it new with you in My Father's kingdom."*
>
> *And when they had sung a hymn, they went out to the Mount of Olives.*
>
> *(Matthew 26:26–30)*

Key Promises in the New Covenant (Ketubah)

Promises to Israel
    A. God Remembers His Covenant with Israel
Promises made to the Church
    B. Remission of Sins and a New Heart
    C. An Everlasting Covenant
    D. Victory over Death
Promises available at Christ's Return
    E. Rule and Reign with Him in His Kingdom
    F. Eternal Life and Our Heavenly Home

A. God Remembers His Covenant with Israel

(See appendix 2, "Kingdom History of Israel and Judah")

God has chosen Israel to be His people through the promises made to Abraham. Paul, from the New Testament, in agreement with God's desire, states:

> *Brethren, my heart's desire and prayer to God for Israel is that they may be saved. For I bear them witness that they have a zeal for God, but not according to knowledge.*
> *(Romans 10:1–2)*

> *And I heard the number of those who were sealed. One hundred and forty-four thousand of all the tribes of the children of Israel were sealed.*
> *(Revelation 7:4)*

Question: The book of Revelation presents a paradox. The paradox is how a remnant of the ten tribes appears in the Tribulation, since their national identity was lost when they were conquered and dispersed by Assyria in 721 BC.

1. God's promise to Israel.
   Deuteronomy 7:6–12
2. The dispersal of Israel (ten tribes) in 721 BC.
   2 Kings 17:19–23
3. God will not cast out all of Israel (a remnant is saved).
   Romans 11:25–29
   Isaiah 59:20-21
4. Both Israel and Judah will be restored by God as one kingdom.
   Hosea 1:10–11
   Ezekiel 37:15–28
   Ezekiel 39:25–29
   Zechariah 10:6
5. God will deliver them in the "Time of Jacob's Trouble."
   Jeremiah 30:7–9
6. The Seed of Abraham (Israel) and Gentile believers have God's blessing.
   Romans 9:23–29
7. The Gospel is not partial.
   Romans 2:8–11

8. Jesus bridges the gap.
   Galatians 3:22–29;
   Romans 3:29–31
9. Both Hebrew and Gentile believers made into one body.[25]
   Ephesians 2:11–16
10. God through Christ makes a "New and Everlasting Covenant."
    Hebrews 8:6–13

B. The Remission of Sins and a New Heart

The sinner is converted when he encounters Christ. "Conversion" means to turn around or turn toward. The bride-to-be, in accepting the terms of the Ketubah, is making the choice to turn her heart toward following her new husband. When we are converted, our lives will begin to reflect our new direction of living for Him. As believers and followers of Christ, we must recognize these most basic truths:

> *Jesus said to him, "I am the way, the truth, and the life. No one comes to the Father except through Me."*
>
> *(John 14:6)*

> *Then Jesus said to His disciples, "If anyone desires to come after Me, let him deny himself, and take up his cross, and follow Me."*
>
> *(Matthew 16:24)*

> *My little children, these things I write to you, so that you may not sin. And if anyone sins, we have an Advocate with the Father, Jesus Christ the righteous. And He Himself is the propitiation for our sins, and not for ours only but also for the whole world.*
>
> *(1 John 2:1–2)*

1. Christ's death on the cross was sufficient to pay for our sins (the bride price) and is authenticated by His resurrection.
   1 Corinthians 15:12–17
2. The Church grows out of the many conversions to faith in Christ.
   Acts 2:46–47
   Acts 4:12
3. We have the full assurance of salvation.
   1 John 5:13

---

25 Salvation by faith does not denigrate the law but fulfills it.

4. We receive a new heart and a new nature.
   Jeremiah 31:33–34
   2 Corinthians 5:17

C. An Everlasting Covenant

When the bridegroom delivers his promises and blessings to his bride-to-be, we can imagine how her heart is filled with joy, as she anticipates what is about to happen in her marriage. Her dreams and hopes are to be fulfilled.

The Beatitudes represent the foundational commandments of the New Covenant. Outward success is a by-product of our inner spiritual achievement. When Jesus delivers these promises and blessings, He conveys the truths to common man. They start so simply: "Blessed are ..."

> Then He opened His mouth and taught them, saying:
> *"Blessed are* the poor in spirit, For theirs is the kingdom of heaven.
> *Blessed are* those who mourn, For they shall be comforted.
> *Blessed are* the meek, For they shall inherit the earth.
> *Blessed are* those who hunger and thirst for righteousness, For they shall be filled.
> *Blessed are* the merciful, For they shall obtain mercy.
> *Blessed are* the pure in heart, For they shall see God.
> *Blessed are* the peacemakers, For they shall be called sons of God.
> *Blessed are* those who are persecuted for righteousness' sake, For theirs is the kingdom of heaven.
> *Blessed are* you when they revile and persecute you, and say all kinds of evil against you falsely for My sake. Rejoice and be exceedingly glad, for great is your reward in heaven, for so they persecuted the prophets who were before you."(Matthew 5:2–12)

There is a sorrow, as Christ tells His disciples that He is about to leave. Yet, there is a joy in being obedient to these principles, as they wait the day of His return and the fulfillment of the promises.

> *Until now you have asked nothing in My name. Ask, and you will receive, that your joy may be full.*
>
> *(John 16:24)*

According to scripture, a person's life is divided into three components or realms: the spirit (spiritual realm that operates by faith), a soul (psychological realm that operates by logic), and a body (physical realm that operates by our senses). By giving us the principles and blessings of the Beatitudes, Christ is directing us toward fulfillment in life. We are then in the process of being "sanctified" in Him, body, soul and spirit, being made ready for our marriage to Him and heaven.

> *Now may the God of peace Himself sanctify you completely; and may your whole spirit, soul, and body be preserved blameless at the coming of our Lord Jesus Christ. He who calls you is faithful, who also will do it.*
> *(1 Thessalonians 5:23–24)*

D. Victory over Death: *Blessed is he, who dies in Christ* [26]

> *Then I heard a voice from heaven saying to me, "Write: 'Blessed are the dead who die in the Lord from now on.'" "Yes," says the Spirit, "that they may rest from their labors, and their works follow them."*
> *(Revelation 14:13)*

The topic of Revelation 14:13 is about those who "die in Christ" during the future Tribulation. I believe that this verse is not limited to the future, but it also pertains to those who have died since Christ's first advent.

Because we tend to think in terms of the physical realm that surrounds us, we are limited in our attempts to understand God's presence. God exists in the spiritual realm. Christ came to His physical creation to redeem us. The physical is finite. God is infinite.

First Corinthians chapter 15 defines the difference between bodies that are made for heaven and bodies made for earth. At our physical death, the spirit and soul of a believer are made ready by Christ to go immediately into Paradise. They receive a *"celestial body"* (1 Corinthians 15:40). Believers should not fear physical death, because it is always the doorway into His presence.

The "Resurrected Body" is what believers receive at the time of Christ's return at the end of the age. Our mortal bodies will *"put on immortality"* (1 Corinthians 15:54).

1. God holds authority over life and death (power to call the dead back to life).
   Deuteronomy 32:39
   Luke 7:12–16
   John 11:42–44
   John 5:21
2. Christ dismissed His Spirit from His body.
   John 10:17–18
   John 19:28–30

---

26 The second of seven blessings listed in Revelation. See appendix 1.

The Groom's Arrival

    3. Before Christ, believers were taken to "the bosom of Abraham."[27]
       Psalm 16:8–11
       Luke 16:22–26

Question: What happens to the righteous who have died since Christ came?

    4. At physical death, the spirit and soul leaves the body of the believer and goes to Paradise.
       Ecclesiastes 12:5–7
       Luke 23:43–46
       John 11:23–26
    5. Believers receive a spiritual body.
       1 Corinthians 15:44
       2 Corinthians 5:6–8
    6. The death of a saint is precious to God (we go home).
       Psalm 72:12–14
       Psalm 116:15

Question:. What will our resurrected body be like?

    7. Jesus took the form of the spiritual (heavenly and resurrected body).
       John 20:17
       1 Corinthians 15:20–23
    8. We will have a resurrected body that is like Christ's at His return.
       Luke 24:36–43
       Romans 6:4–5
       1 Corinthians 15:45–49
       Revelation 21:3–7
    9. Our spiritual and resurrected body will become one.
       2 Corinthians 12:1–4
       John 20:26–29
    10. Our desire (now) is to be with Christ and God in our eternal state.
       2 Corinthians 5:9–10
       Philippians 1:20–23

E. Rule and Reign with Him in His Kingdom

    God's promise to Israel:

---

[27] A figure of speech for heaven from the Talmud.

> "Now therefore, if you will indeed obey My voice and keep My covenant, then you shall be a special treasure to Me above all people; for all the earth is Mine. And you shall be to Me a kingdom of priests and a holy nation." These are the words which you shall speak to the children of Israel.
>
> *(Exodus 19:5–6)*

God's promise to the Church:

> And from Jesus Christ, the faithful witness, the firstborn from the dead, and the ruler over the kings of the earth. To Him who loved us and washed us from our sins in His own blood, and has made us kings and priests to His God and Father, to Him be glory and dominion forever and ever. Amen.
>
> *(Revelation 1:5–6)*

> But you (gentile believers) are a chosen generation, a royal priesthood, a holy nation, His own special people, that you may proclaim the praises of Him who called you out of darkness into His marvelous light; who once were not a people but are now the people of God, who had not obtained mercy but now have obtained mercy.
>
> *(1 Peter 2:9–10)*

1. Christ is the creator of all things. All things belong to Him.
   Colossians 1:16–17
2. Christ's Kingdom is for both heaven and the earth.
   Revelation 11:15
3. His Kingdom is made up of both Hebrew and Gentile believers.
   Luke 1:31–33
   Romans 15:8–12
   Ephesians 3:6–7

F. Eternal Life and Our Heavenly Home

Blessed are those who do His commandments[28]

> Blessed are those who do His commandments, that they may have the right to the tree of life, and may enter through the gates into the city.
>
> *(Revelation 22:14)*

---

[28] The seventh of seven blessings listed in Revelation. See appendix 1. The Greek New Testament translates "do His commandments" as "wash their robes."

1. Life in the presence of God.
   a. With Adam in the beginning.
      Genesis 2:15–25
   b. At the time of Moses.
      Exodus 20:18–21
   c. The fear of the Lord (came because of Adam's sin).
      Genesis 3:8–10
      Job 28:28
      Philippians 2:12–13
   d. Boldness to enter God's presence through Christ.
      Hebrews 10:19–22
2. The trees in God's Garden.
   a. Eden and the trees, God's Covenant with Adam.
      Genesis 2:8–9
      Genesis 2:15
   b. The knowledge of good and evil, disobedience and death.
      Genesis 2:16–17
      1 Corinthians 15:21–22
   c. The lust of the flesh and leaving God's presence.
      Genesis 3:22–23
      1 John 2:16
   d. Obedience and finding the "Tree of Life."
      Proverbs 3:13–18
      Revelation 2:7
3. Our citizenship in heaven.
   Ephesians 2:18–19
   Hebrews 11:14–16
4. The gates of the City.
   a. There is an angel guarding the gates of Paradise.
      Genesis 3:24
      Matthew 7:13–14
   b. Our access to the city is granted through Christ.
      John 10:1–4
      John 14:6
      Psalm 118:19–20

Chapter 9

Matan, The Bridal Gift

> ### *Matan, the Bridal Gift* (Betrothal Ring)
> At the time of the groom's departure, he would give his wife-to-be a special gift, or *matan,* as a pledge of his love. A betrothal ring was often used as a public sign of their covenant. The gift was to serve as a reminder to her during their days of separation. He would then leave with these words, "I go to prepare a place for you." At this point, the two were by law husband and wife. In the ancient tradition, the betrothed bride would begin to wear a veil over her face in public as a sign of the betrothal.

A. "Firstfruits" and the Promise of a Harvest

Jewish adult men were required to attend three festivals annually (Exodus 34:22–24). These feasts[29] were connected to their agrarian heritage and celebrated the barley, wheat and fruit harvests.

The Feast of Passover in April celebrated the (early) barley harvest. Christ is the firstfruit of the resurrection and is God's model for the resurrection of those who are redeemed.

The later Feast of Pentecost coincided with the June wheat harvest. It is the duplication of the Old Testament celebration established by God in the Festival of Weeks. In the New Testament, the word "Pentecost" is the Greek word for fiftieth. It is held fifty days after Passover.

In the wedding tradition the giving of the betrothal ring is symbolic of the giving of the Holy Spirit to the Church at Pentecost. We become "sealed" with the Holy Spirit as a sign of our betrothal to Christ. We become a part

---

29 *The MacArthur Study Bible,* pages 185-186, commentary on Jewish Feasts in Leviticus chapter 23.

of the "firstfruits" of God's harvest at the end of the age and Christ's return for His Church.

When Jesus leaves, He promises to the disciples that He will allow the *"Helper"* (in Greek, p*arakletos,* John 14:16) to come and be present with them during His absence. In John 14:18 Jesus says, *"I will not leave you orphans, I will come to you."* He continues His promise in John 14:20 where He says, *"At that day you will know that I am in the Father, and you in Me, and I in you."* The Holy Spirit "*in you"* is to be a constant reminder of His love and promise to return.

> *And being assembled together with them, He commanded them not to depart from Jerusalem, but to wait for the Promise of the Father, "which," He said, "you have heard from Me; for John truly baptized with water, but you shall be baptized with the Holy Spirit not many days from now."*
>
> *(Acts 1:4–5)*

> *Therefore, when they had come together, they asked Him, saying, "Lord, will You at this time restore the kingdom to Israel?" And He said to them, "It is not for you to know times or seasons which the Father has put in His own authority."*
>
> *(Acts 1:6–7)*

B. The Promised Gift of the Holy Spirit

1. God's promise of the Holy Spirit.
   Joel 2:28–29
   Acts 1:8
   Acts 2:16–21
2. Jesus tells us about the Holy Spirit.
   John 14:15–17
   John 14:25–26
   John 16:13–14
3. John's Baptism[30] and the Baptism with the Holy Spirit.
   Luke 3:16
   Acts 2:38–41

---

30 See the section on Mikveh, chapter 6.

C. The Bride Receives the Betrothal Guarantee

1. The Holy Spirit is the guarantee[31] (seal) of our betrothal.
   Ephesians 1:13–14
   2 Corinthians 1:21–22
   2 Corinthians 5:5–7
2. The gift to the Church, Baptism in the Holy Spirit.[32]
   Acts 8:14-17
   Acts 10:44-48
   1 Corinthians 12:12–14
   Galatians 3:14
3. The arrival of the Holy Spirit and the day of Pentecost.
   Deuteronomy 16:9–12
   Acts 2:1–4

---

31 The word "guarantee" in Ephesians 1:14, from the Greek, is also used as the word in connection with a betrothal ring.
32 The gift of the Holy Spirit is examined in "Eyrusin, the Betrothal," chapter 10.

Chapter 10
Eyrusin, The Betrothal

> ### *Eyrusin, the Betrothal*
>
> In Hebrew tradition, the betrothal period, or *eyrusin*, could be up to a year or more. The word *kinddushin* stands for the time period of the *eyrusin*, or betrothal, and means "sanctification" or "set apart." It is a time when the couple prepare themselves. They are legally married to each other under the terms of the betrothal contract. They continue to live separately and remain chaste throughout the betrothal period.
>
> On his return home, the groom begins the task of adding rooms (*chador*, chambers) to his father's house. He promises that when the rooms are finished, he will return for her. He is anxious to claim his bride, but his father, on the other hand, would restrain his son's enthusiasm until all of the tasks of preparation were complete. If the young man were to be asked when the day of his wedding was to take place, he would say, "No man knows the day or the hour; only my father knows."
>
> The bride goes about her day-to-day tasks but with an eye toward the day her husband-to-be returns. Her focus is all about preparations for the marriage. The bride and her household must always be prepared, as they do not know the time or day of his return.

A. The Betrothal and the Bride—Finding Her Purpose

We are saved by His grace, but we have a calling to live as one who is betrothed to the King of Kings. In a sense, the true Church is legally "married" to Christ. It should be abhorrent when we are willfully unfaithful. To be unfaithful is like the act of adultery. When we sin, our fellowship is broken, and there is a need for repentance and restoration. He is always ready for restoration.

For the Bride, it is a time of preparation. Here are some of her tasks:
1. To love her Lord and His appearance.
   John 14:21
   Ephesians 3:14–19
2. To love others.
   John 13:34–35
3. To obey and serve.
   John 15:9–14
4. To teach others.
   Acts 5:42
5. To glorify her Lord.
   John 15:8
6. To wait patiently for her Lord's return.
   Romans 8:22–25

B. The Betrothal and Christ

God the Father loves us through His Son. In looking at the betrothal through the eyes of the wedding tradition, we are like God's daughter-in-law or son-in-law. We are married to Christ. We are God's children and part of His family. From the moment we receive the Holy Spirit, we are sealed in Him and are a legal heir to all of the promises of the Father. He does not go back on His Word.

C. The Bride and the Church Age

For the Church, the Betrothal period began with the Ascension of Christ into heaven from the Mount of Olives and the giving of the Holy Spirit at the Day of Pentecost. This was the start of the "Church Age."

And Jesus came and spoke to them, saying, "All authority has been given to Me in heaven and on earth. Go therefore and make disciples of all the nations, baptizing them in the name of the Father and of the Son and of the Holy Spirit, teaching them to observe all things that I have commanded you; and lo, I am with you always, even to the end of the age." Amen.
(Matthew 28:18–20)

"But you shall receive power when the Holy Spirit has come upon you; and you shall be witnesses to Me in Jerusalem, and in all Judea and Samaria, and to the end of the earth." Now when He had spoken these things, while they watched, He was taken up, and a cloud received Him out of their sight.

(Acts 1:8–9)

The Church begins to grow by the empowerment of lives through the Holy Spirit. It spreads out from Jerusalem. At first, Paul is a persecutor of the Church. His encounter with the resurrected Jesus on the road to Damascus changes all of that. He is transformed by Christ and becomes the messenger of God to the Gentile nations.

In all of the days since Pentecost, the Church has been in preparation for the Lord's return. He has left us with the Holy Spirit to equip and empower us. Jesus Christ, the Groom, awaits in heaven for His Father to signal the day for His return. He has been busy preparing our eternal home for over nineteen hundred years. The *chuppah*, or bridal chamber, will be a wondrous place beyond our imagination.

> *Eye has not seen, nor ear heard, nor has it entered into the heart of man the things that God has prepared for those who love Him.*
> *(1 Corinthians.2:9)*

D. The Church and the Holy Spirit (Sanctification)

The Church is not perfect but is in the process of transformation. Our position is that we are seen by God through the perfection of His Son. We do not have to become perfect, but we are to live under the power of the grace granted to us through God's Word and the redemption given us through Christ. As a practical matter, the Church is to yield to the Holy Spirit's transformative power. The Holy Spirit is at work to purify and transform those who are the Bride of Christ. We are to be ready to commit our mind and will over to Christ.

1. Holy Communication: Prayer and what you hear from God.
   a. The role of The Holy Spirit and Christ in our prayers.
      Romans 8:26–27
      1 Corinthians 2:10–12
   b. The power of prayer that is based in God's will.
      1 John 5:14–15
   c. Jesus gives us His name to use.
      John 14:12–14
      John 15:16
   d. Ask and believe through faith.
      Matthew 7:7–8
   e. Ask with right motives.
      Matthew 6:5–6
      James 4:1–3
   f. Jesus' model prayer.
      Matthew 6:9–13

2. Holy Conduct: What you do in God's Kingdom.
      a. We are called to be holy in our conduct.
         2 Corinthians 7:1
      b. Salvation brings a change of heart.
         Titus 2:14
      c. As "bond servants," we are voluntarily dedicated to God.
         Exodus 21:2, 5–6
         Romans 12:1–2
      d. Our faith journey is to "go on to perfection."[33]
         Matthew 5:48
         Hebrews 6:1–3
   3. Holy Character: Walking in the Spirit, where you go.
      a. We are to be filled with the Holy Spirit.
         Ephesians 5:17–21
      b. We are commanded to "Walk in the Spirit."
         Isaiah 30:21
         Galatians 5:16–26

Being filled with the Holy Spirit is one step beyond being sealed with the Holy Spirit (Ephesians 1:13). Not all true Christians are spirit filled, but all are spirit sealed. Being filled leads the believer to acts of praise, worship, and service. When the scripture says, "Walk in the Spirit," we are being instructed to be filled.

E. The Gift of the Holy Spirit

The Holy Spirit empowers the Church in the extension and growth of God's Kingdom on earth during the time of Christ's preparation in heaven. Christ has not left us alone to struggle under our own power while we await His return.

There are three distinct Greek words that are translated into the English word "gift." *Charismata* is used for the personal gifts given to an individual believer. *Doma* is used to indicate the corporate gifts functioning in a church. *Phanerosis* is used when the Holy Spirit intercedes at a particular time and for a particular need. All three gift categories are listed in 1 Corinthians 12:4 where it states *"there are diversities of gifts, but the same Spirit"*.

   1. Listing of Gifts.
      a. *Charismata*   1 Corinthians 12:5   Romans 12:6–8
      b. *Doma*   1 Corinthians 12:6   Ephesians 4:7-13
      c. *Phanerosis*   1 Corinthians 12:7   1 Corinthians 12:7–11

---

[33] This doctrine of sanctification was emphasized by John Wesley and others during the Great Awakening of the 1700s.

2. We are chosen to be blessed with spiritual gifts.
   1 Corinthians 12:1–4
   Ephesians 1:3–6
3. Jesus empowers the Church through the Holy Spirit.
   Luke 24:46–49
   2 Corinthians 4:6–7
4. The transforming power of the Holy Spirit.
   a. The power as our teacher.
      1 John 2:20, 27
      1 John 5:6
   b. Power to witness.
      Isaiah 43:10–12
      Acts 4:29–31
   c. Power to overcome evil and demonic forces.
      1 John 4:4
      1 John 5:4–5
      Matthew 10:1
   d. The Holy Spirit is given to equip the saints in battle.
      Joshua 1:9–11
      Psalm 27:1–3
      Ephesians 6:10–13
   e. Power to overcome death.
      John 8:51
      Romans 6:9
5. "Spiritual gifts" are to be used, awaiting His coming.
   1 Corinthians 1:4–8

Chapter 11
Nisuin, The Presentation

> ### Nisuin, the Presentation
>
> The word *nisuin* means to "lift up" or "carry." After completion of the new home and at a time determined by the groom's father, the groom and his friends would assemble and proceed to the bride's parent's home. The groom designates two close friends (witnesses) to assist him. The witnesses attest to the fulfillment of his marriage covenant promises.
>
> The bride would not know the day or time of his return. The groom's procession would usually start at dusk with torches, shouts, and trumpets (*shofar*) that could be seen and heard leading them across the hillsides. He would claim his bride. At this point, the bride would be lifted up and carried on the shoulders of the groom's procession as they return to his father's home for the marriage ceremony. The temporary canopy, representing the *chuppah*, would be raised over her during the procession. There was a strict observance that only those with proper invitations were allowed to attend the ceremony.

The Church is waiting for the Groom's arrival. John the Baptist acted as a witness at Christ's fist advent. John called himself "Friend of the Bridegroom" (John 3:27–29). There will be two witnesses like John the Baptist, who will call for repentance and the coming judgment during the Great Tribulation.

> *For they themselves declare concerning us what manner of entry we had to you, and how you turned to God from idols to serve the living and true God, and to wait for His Son from heaven, whom He raised from the dead, even Jesus who delivers us from the wrath to come.*
>
> *(1 Thessalonians 1:9–10)*

It is clear from scripture that Jesus will deliver us, *"from the wrath to come."* We do not know the day or the hour of His arrival. Being ready and prepared is the task of the true Church. He is looking for the "righteous Bride" with which to share His Kingdom. When He comes, He will "lift up" and "carry" the Bride to heaven. The arrival will be preceded with a shout and a trumpet call in a moment in time.

> *For this we say to you by the word of the Lord, that we who are alive and remain until the coming of the Lord will by no means precede those who are asleep. For the Lord Himself will descend from heaven with a shout, with the voice of an archangel, and with the trumpet of God. And the dead in Christ will rise first. Then we who are alive and remain shall be caught up together with them in the clouds to meet the Lord in the air. And thus we shall always be with the Lord. Therefore comfort one another with these words.*
>
> *(1 Thessalonians 4:15–18)*

A. *Blessed is he who watches and keeps his garments*[34]

> *Behold, I am coming as a thief. Blessed is he who watches, and keeps his garments, lest he walk naked and they see his shame.*
>
> *(Revelation 16:15)*

The Harpazo Effect

The Greek word *harpazo* means caught up and it pertains to being seized or plucked up by force. The word is used in 1 Thessalonians 4:17 for when the Church is suddenly removed from earth. At Christ's return, the saints are immediately transformed from mortal to immortal (1 Corinthians 15:42–45).

There is no better illustration of waiting with the expectation of His return than the one given by our Lord in the parable of the ten virgins.

> *Then the kingdom of heaven shall be likened to ten virgins who took their lamps and went out to meet the bridegroom. Now five of them were wise, and five were foolish. Those who were foolish took their lamps and took no oil with them, but the wise took oil in their vessels with their lamps. But while the bridegroom was delayed, they all slumbered and slept.*
>
> *And at midnight a cry was heard: "Behold, the bridegroom is coming; go out to meet him!" Then all those virgins arose and trimmed their lamps. And the foolish said to the wise, "Give us some of your oil, for our lamps are going*

---

[34] The third of seven blessings listed in Revelation. See appendix 1.

out." But the wise answered, saying, "No, lest there should not be enough for us and you; but go rather to those who sell, and buy for yourselves." And while they went to buy, the bridegroom came, and those who were ready went in with him to the wedding; and the door was shut.

Afterward the other virgins came also, saying, "Lord, Lord, open to us!" But he answered and said, "Assuredly, I say to you, I do not know you." Watch therefore, for you know neither the day nor the hour in which the Son of Man is coming.

(Matthew 25:1–13)

Question: Why should we live expecting the Lord's return?

1. Conditions on earth.
   Matthew 24:4–8
2. "Behold I am coming like a thief" (Revelation 16:15a).
   Matthew 24:27
   1 Thessalonians 5:1–4
3. We are to be ready at all times.
   Matthew 24:36-39
   Luke 17:20–24

Let your waist be girded and your lamps burning; and you yourselves be like men who wait for their master, when he will return from the wedding, that when he comes and knocks they may open to him immediately. Blessed are those servants whom the master, when he comes, will find watching. Assuredly, I say to you that he will gird himself and have them sit down to eat, and will come and serve them ... Therefore you also be ready, for the Son of Man is coming at an hour you do not expect.

(Luke 12:35–37, 40)

Question: When does the "Rapture" take place?

1. At a time set by God the Father.
   Mark 13:32
   Acts 1:6–7
2. When the "man of sin is revealed."
   2 Thessalonians 2:1–4
3. Believers will be "saved" at His appearance.
   1 Thessalonians 1:10
   1 John 2:28

John Cooper

Question: What is the "Day of Christ"?

The "Day of Jesus Christ" and the "Day of Christ" are different from the "Day of the Lord." The Day of the Lord pertains to Christ's return to earth as the conquering king at the end of the Great Tribulation, when He enters the final battle.

I believe the phrase the "Day of Jesus Christ" refers to the taking of the Bride to her new home at the start of the Tribulation. When we see this event through the wedding tradition of *nisuin*, our vision and understanding improves.

Some propose that the timing of the rapture of the Church may coincide with the Jewish celebration of *Rosh Hashanah*, which means "head of the year". The agricultural and secular year began with this celebration and was also called the "Feast of Trumpets" or a "Day of the Blowing of the Trumpet". (Leviticus 23:23–38).

Rosh Hashanah is celebrated as the start of each new year (September/October) and represents a new beginning for the Jewish people. In their tradition, it celebrates the anniversary of God's creation of the world. It begins a ten-day period of reflection and repentance. Each person is expected to take an inventory of the soul. The days were also called *Yom Hadin*, the Days of Repentance. Jews are instructed to picture God as King, sitting on the Throne of Judgment.

At the end of the ten days, Rosh Hashanah is followed by *Yom Kippur, or* the Day of Atonement. It is observed annually to atone for the sins of the nation both corporately and individually. It is ironic that the word "sin" is not found in the Hebrew language but is taken from the word *chet*, which literally means to "miss the mark" or "veer off course." At *Yom Kippur*, a Hebrew man might wear a pure white robe called a *kittel* to signify cleansing and purity. It is interesting that the groom wears a *kittel* at his wedding. *Yom Kippur* is a High Holy Day of the calendar.

1. Discerning the times.
   Luke 12:54–56
2. We are to be found faithful at His appearance.
   1 Corinthians 1:6–8
   Philippians 1:3–6
   Philippians 1:9–11
   Philippians 2:14–16
3. True believers, the Bride of Christ, "Raptured."
   1 Thessalonians 4:13–18
   John 6:39–40
   John 14:1–4
   1 Corinthians 15:51–52

4. Persecution of those who remain on earth.
   Daniel 12:1
   Revelation 6:9–11

After the Rapture of the Church (the Bride), many on the earth will come to realize their need to repent and come to a saving relationship with Christ. Many assumed their previous faith was true but, like the Church at Laodicea, now see what they have missed. Salvation will continue to be extended but only through the events of the Tribulation.

At the same time as the Rapture, Satan convinces his followers to believe that his path to rule and control the realm of earth is clear. The Holy Spirit's restraining power through the true Church has been removed. The restraint of his power and demonic influence is no longer in place; therefore, he seeks to destroy and exercise control over any who might stand in his way.

> *Then one of the elders answered, saying to me, "Who are these arrayed in white robes, and where did they come from?" And I said to him, "Sir, you know." So he said to me, "These are the ones who come out of the great tribulation, and washed their robes and made them white in the blood of the Lamb."*
>
> (Revelation 7:13–14)

The Word does not promise to separate all believers from the suffering and martyrdom to come. There will be others who hear the message of the Good News and come to Christ for salvation during the Tribulation. God's plan is to include these people in His Kingdom. They will be brought home at the "Tribulation Harvest" (chapter 12) just prior to the outpouring of God's final wrath on the earth.

Question: How should we properly prepare for His coming?

1. OT[35] custom of providing proper garments.
   Genesis 41:39–43
   Esther 6:6–11
2. God supplies the garments for Israel.
   Ezekiel 16:9–14
3. Clothed in our own righteousness?
   Matthew 5:20
   Romans 3:10–12

---

[35] To meet with the King and participate in activities of the court, the King's guests were provided garments, so they would be properly attired for the royal occasion.

4. God will supply the garments of righteousness.
   Romans 5:8–10
5. God sees the righteousness of Christ.
   Colossians 1:27–28
   Romans 5:19–21

B. Our Reward at His Appearance

At Christ's return, the believers will be recognized for their faithfulness regarding the stewardship of the life God has given them. At the *bema*, Judgment Seat of Jesus Christ, believers are recognized. For them, this is an awards ceremony to be looked forward to, not a judgment to be feared. Christ has already rendered the payment for our sins. This scripture points to the fact that our rewards occur at our resurrection and Christ's coming for His Church. It is not at our physical death as some suggest.

> *And behold, I am coming quickly, and My reward is with Me, to give to everyone according to his work. I am the Alpha and the Omega, the Beginning and the End, the First and the Last.*
> *(Revelation 22:12–13)*

> *For the Son of Man will come in the glory of His Father with His angels, and then He will reward each according to his works.*
> *(Matthew 16:27)*

1. Our reward is with Him.
   Isaiah 62:11–12
   Psalm 18:20–24
2. The Judgment Seat of Jesus Christ.
   2 Timothy 4:8
   1 Corinthians 4:3–5
3. Rewards according to each one's work.
   Matthew 16:27–28
   2 Corinthians 5:9–11
   2 Timothy 4:18
4. Dealing with remaining carnality.
   Romans 8:5–13
   Hebrews 5:12–14

Chapter 12
Chuppah, The Bridal Chamber and Ceremony

Chuppah, Bridal Chamber, and Ceremony

This tradition was much more than just a short ceremony and a meal with the guests. It usually included seven full days of activity and celebration. Only properly invited guests were allowed. The sequence of events during the wedding was: 1. ceremony, 2. seclusion of the bride and groom, and 3. the marriage supper.

The custom of lifting the bride and groom on chairs is a part of the processional. The bride's chair is covered with a canopy representing the *chuppah*, or bridal chamber. The groom and his bride are regarded as without blemish, and they are seen as king and queen of the celebration. At one point, the bride walks or dances around the groom seven times, with her eyes strictly on him as her king. The groom wears a white garment called a *kittel*. The bride wears a veil, which symbolizes her modesty and purity.

The groom's father is joyful, as he recognizes that his eldest son will continue the family linage. The guests pay homage to the father of the groom. They rejoice over the marriage. The gift of a bride for his son fills the father's heart with joy. The father brings to the groom and his new bride the blessings of his inheritance. He blesses the marriage and looks forward to the day when he will be blessed again with his children's children.

The father's son has been publicly proclaimed "faithful and worthy" by his fulfillment of the promises made at the beginning of the *eyrusin*, or betrothal. Following the final reading and second signing of the *ketubah*, the Marriage Covenant is sealed with the sharing and drinking of a second "Covenant Cup of Acceptance."

The words of the wedding ceremony are taken from Psalm 45 and Isaiah 61:10 through 62:5. These are the traditional vows of love as expressed in God's love for Israel. The ceremony concludes with a sevenfold blessing called the *brachot*, given by the presiding rabbi.

The groom and the bride then proceed to the actual bridal chamber to consummate their relationship. The doors are locked from the inside.

The Father's Gift: Revelation Chapter 4

> *After these things I looked, and behold, a door standing open in heaven. And the first voice which I heard was like a trumpet speaking with me, saying, "Come up here, and I will show you things which must take place after this."*
> *Immediately I was in the Spirit; and behold, a throne set in heaven, and One sat on the throne.*
> *(Revelation 4:1–2)*

Beginning with Revelation chapter 4, John sees the open door of heaven and the throne with the presence of God where the wedding ceremony is to take place.

A. Invited Guests Only

> *On the third day there was a wedding in Cana of Galilee, and the mother of Jesus was there. Now both Jesus and His disciples were invited to the wedding.*
> *(John 2:1–2)*

> *But when the king came in to see the guests, he saw a man there who did not have on a wedding garment. So he said to him, "Friend, how did you come in here without a wedding garment?" And he was speechless. Then the king said to the servants, "Bind him hand and foot, take him away, and cast him into outer darkness; there will be weeping and gnashing of teeth."*
> *For many are called, but few are chosen.*
> *(Matthew 22:11–14)*

B. An Inheritance and a Harvest

> *The twenty-four elders fall down before Him who sits on the throne and worship Him who lives forever and ever, and cast their crowns before the throne, saying: "You are worthy, O Lord, To receive glory and honor and power; For You created all things, And by Your will they exist and were created."*
> *(Revelation 4:10-11)*

> *He who overcomes shall inherit all things, and I will be his God and he shall be My son.*
> *(Revelation 21:7)*

God's gift, the inheritance of this world, is to be delivered into Christ's hands. Only Jesus is allowed to take the scroll and break the seals to start the process. Christ will redeem those who are His. Tribulation and judgment will come at the end of the age to cleanse the earth and make it ready for Jesus' reign.

Blessed is he who keeps the words of the prophesy.

> *Then he said to me, "These words are faithful and true." And the Lord God of the holy prophets sent His angel to show His servants the things which must shortly take place. "Behold, I am coming quickly! Blessed is he who keeps the words of the prophecy of this book."*[36]
> *(Revelation 22:6–7)*

Christ has been "faithful and true" to His Father's commands. He has fulfilled the covenant promises. By fulfilling the prophesies and the promises of God, Christ has proven Himself to be the "Worthy One" and to claim the Church, open the seals of judgment, reclaim the earth, and receive His Father's Kingdom.

1. God's character and Word are faithful and true.
   Deuteronomy 7:7–9
   Psalm 19:7–11
2. Jesus comes as faith and truth incarnate.
   John 7:16–18
   Hebrews 3:1–6
   1 Thessalonians 5:23–24

We are told in Matthew 6:19, *"Do not lay up for yourselves treasures on earth, where moth and rust destroy and where thieves break in and steal."* Our earthly fathers may give us an inheritance that is temporal and lasts but a season, whereas our Heavenly Father is giving us an inheritance that is irrevocable and eternal.

> *The Spirit Himself bears witness with our spirit that we are children of God, and if children, then heirs—heirs of God and joint heirs with Christ, if indeed we suffer with Him, that we may also be glorified together.*
> *(Romans 8:16–17)*

that in the dispensation of the fullness of the times He might gather together in one all things in Christ, both which are in heaven and which

---

36 The sixth of seven blessings listed in Revelation. See appendix 1.

are on earth—in Him. In Him also we have obtained an inheritance, being predestined according to the purpose of Him who works all things according to the counsel of His will, that we who first trusted in Christ should be to the praise of His glory.

(Ephesians 1:10-12)

The Tribulation Harvest of the earth takes place near the end of the Great Tribulation. Before the wedding supper, God delivers an inheritance of blessings to the faithful as He fulfills the promises of His covenant with the Bride of His Son. Those who have denied the Son receive a harvest of God's wrath.

Another parable He put forth to them, saying: "The kingdom of heaven is like a man who sowed good seed in his field; but while men slept, his enemy came and sowed tares among the wheat and went his way. But when the grain had sprouted and produced a crop, then the tares also appeared. So the servants of the owner came and said to him, 'Sir, did you not sow good seed in your field? How then does it have tares?' He said to them, 'An enemy has done this.' The servants said to him, 'Do you want us then to go and gather them up?' But he said, 'No, lest while you gather up the tares you also uproot the wheat with them. Let both grow together until the harvest, and at the time of harvest I will say to the reapers, First gather together the tares and bind them in bundles to burn them, but gather the wheat into my barn.'"

(Matthew 13:24–30)

Then the seventh angel sounded: And there were loud voices in heaven, saying, "The kingdoms of this world have become the kingdoms of our Lord and of His Christ, and He shall reign forever and ever!"

(Revelation 11:15)

Jesus Opens the Scroll: Revelation Chapter 5

A. The Scroll[37]

And I saw in the right hand of Him who sat on the throne a scroll written inside and on the back, sealed with seven seals. Then I saw a strong angel proclaiming with a loud voice, "Who is worthy to open the scroll and to loose its seals?"

(Revelation 5:1–2)

---

37 The description of a scroll in Zachariah 5:2 is twenty by ten cubits, or thirty by fifteen feet. How large is the one in Revelation chapter 5?

Beginning with Revelation chapter 5, and as the final act of fulfilling the promises of God's inheritance, Jesus opens the scroll and breaks the seals. With the breaking of the seals, God is granting Christ the right to full dominion over the earth. Satan will be cast out and bound; Jesus will reign. Breaking the seals releases the "Host of Heaven," the Army of God, as Christ begins the final steps of completing God's plan.

1. The One who has the "Key of David."
   Revelation 3:7
   Revelation 5:4–5
2. The "Redeemer."
   Revelation 5:9–10
   Titus 2:11-14
3. Honor to the Father; honor to the Son.
   Revelation 5:12–13
   Revelation 7:9–10
4. The scroll and the "curse."
   Zechariah 5:1–4
   Ezekiel 2:9-10

B. Understanding the Scroll

Now as He sat on the Mount of Olives, the disciples came to Him privately, saying, "Tell us, when will these things be? And what will be the sign of Your coming, and of the end of the age?"

(Matthew 24:3)

Eschatology and timelines applied to the book of Revelation are among the most difficult to interpret and are subject to a widely variable school of thought. In connecting Revelation, Matthew, Daniel, and the marriage tradition, it is my prayer the reader will see the meaningful relationships and the plan God has for the Church. Jesus, in His Olivet Discourse, establishes a prophetic framework for all other biblical prophesies concerning His return. In a sense Jesus is using the equivalent of *Cliff's Notes* to help us comprehend the content of the other scriptures pertaining to His return.

Olivet Discourse Timeline, Matthew chapters 24–25: *See appendix 4.*

#1 Pre-Tribulation	Matthew 24:4–8
#2 Tribulation Starts	Matthew 24:9–14
#3 Abomination of Desolation	Matthew 24:15
#4 The Great Tribulation	Matthew 24:16–21

#5 Tribulation Harvest	Matthew 24:36–44
#6 The Wrath of God	Matthew 24:22
#7 The Day of the Lord	Matthew 24:27–31
#8 The Earth Is Cleansed	Matthew 24:45–51
#9 The Marriage of the Lamb	Matthew 25:1–13
#10 The Millennial Reign of Christ	Matthew 25:14–46

Matthew 24:15 ties together the "abomination of desolation" with the verses of Daniel 9:27, 11:31, and 12:11. Furthermore, it anchors the midpoint of the "Days of Daniel" and establishes a beginning, middle, and end of the age.

C. Days of Daniel (*1,260, 1,290, and 1,335, appendix 4*)

Daniel is like no other Old Testament prophet when he sets a prophetic timeline. In the, "sixty-two plus seven weeks" (69 weeks of years or 483 years) of Daniel 9:24–25, he lays out the exact days of Nehemiah's rebuilding of Jerusalem and the coming of the Christ on Palm Sunday as the Messiah. Scholars have placed the historical timeline as beginning on March 14, 445 BC with the writing of the decree for the rebuilding of the temple, and ending with Jesus' arrival into Jerusalem on Palm Sunday, April 6, AD 32: 483 prophetic years of 360 days each, to the exact day.[38]

Daniel 12:6–7 defines the final three and a half years, or 1,260 days, to "finish" the (Great) Tribulation. In an identical form, Revelation 11:1–3, 12:6, and 13:5 define the Great Tribulation as 42 months, or 1,260 days.

The Tribulation events at the end of Daniel's prophecy (12:11–13) have always had the appearance of being left out of other timelines. Daniel was instructed to seal the words of his prophecy until the time of the end. John is instructed to keep Revelation "unsealed." Jesus, in Matthew and Revelation, is giving us keys to help open and understand Daniel's prophecies. Question: Is the scroll that was sealed in Daniel the same one that Jesus now opens?

> *Although I heard, I did not understand. Then I said, "My lord, what shall be the end of these things?"*
> *And he said, "Go your way, Daniel, for the words are closed up and sealed till the time of the end."*
>
> (Daniel 12:8–9)

> *And he said to me, "Do not seal the words of the prophecy of this book, for the time is at hand."*
>
> (Revelation 22:10)

---

38 From "Daniels Prophecy of the Seventy Weeks," by Dr. Alva J. McClain, 1970, pp. 19–22.

The wedding tradition order of *ceremony, seclusion,* and *marriage supper* helps us to frame the final timelines in Matthew and Revelation in sequence. The Marriage Supper of the Lamb forms the final point in the chronology that will end with Daniel's day 1,335. The Marriage Supper of the Lamb occurs after the Day of the Lord, day 1,290, and before day 1,335. I believe that the "inheritance" of Daniel 12:12 on day 1,335 represents the start of Christ's Millennial Reign on earth.

> *And from the time that the daily sacrifice is taken away, and the abomination of desolation is set up, there shall be one thousand two hundred and ninety days. Blessed is he who waits, and comes to the one thousand three hundred and thirty-five days.*
> *But you, go your way till the end; for you shall rest, and will arise to your inheritance at the end of the days.*
>
> *(Daniel 12:11–13)*

The events of days 1,260 and 1,290 are defined in later sections of this chapter. By looking at the sequencing of these days through the ancient Hebrew tradition, God allows us to see more clearly the events that will surround Jesus' return.

The Contents of the Scroll: Revelation Chapters 6 through 18

A. Tribulation Seals Opened: Revelation Chapters 6 and 13

(*Day 1,260 to Abomination of Desolation, Appendix 4*)

> *Now I saw when the Lamb opened one of the seals; and I heard one of the four living creatures saying with a voice like thunder, "Come and see."*
>
> *(Revelation 6:1)*

The power of restraint has been secured by the Holy Spirit during the Church Age. At the start of tribulation, the restraint is withdrawn. These events also represent the result of what happens at the removal (rapture) of the Church. The "Beast Out of the Sea," or antichrist, begins his world domination and control. The "Four Horsemen," or apocalyptical forces, symbolize the areas of the battles that intensify and begin to take place over the realm of earth.

The Tribulation begins when Jesus opens the first seal. The "White Horse" represents the antichrist and his influence. He will deceive many. In coming to the world stage, he miraculously makes a peace agreement with the Jews and other world leaders that lasts for three and one-half years. The treaty allows the Jews to reestablish temple worship in Jerusalem. For them, it seems like a dream come true. In fact, it is a deception formed in the halls of hell. Many others will follow Satan's plan. War, famine, and death will follow. The worst is yet to come.

1. The Beast Out of the Sea (antichrist).
   Revelation 13:1–10
2. The Beast Out of the Earth (false prophet).
   Revelation 13:11–18
3. Seals One–Four of the Apocalypse.
   Revelation 6:1–8
   Zechariah 1:7–11
   a. First Seal: the White Horse, false peace, and the prince that shall come.
      Revelation 6:2
      Daniel 9:27
   b. Second Seal: the Red Horse, the one who takes peace and makes war.
      Revelation 6:3-4
      Matthew 24:6–8
   c. Third Seal: the Black Horse, economic breakdown, and political control.
      Revelation 6:5–6
      Joel 1:10–15
   d. Fourth Seal: the Pale Horse, the power to kill one-fourth of all mankind.
      Revelation 6:8
      Ezekiel 18:30–32
      2 Corinthians 2:15–16
4. Fifth Seal: souls of the righteous martyrs.
   Revelation 6:9–11
5. Sixth Seal: great calamity; the lost seek to hide themselves.
   Revelation 6:12–17

B. Satan Is Cast out of Heaven: Revelation 12:7–13

(Abomination of Desolation, Appendix 4)

And war broke out in heaven: Michael and his angels fought with the dragon; and the dragon and his angels fought, but they did not prevail, nor was a place found for them in heaven any longer. So the

great dragon was cast out, that serpent of old, called the Devil and Satan, who deceives the whole world; he was cast to the earth, and his angels were cast out with him.
(Revelation 12:7–9)

The Great Tribulation starts at the midpoint of the seven-year period. Satan and the (demonic) angels that follow him are barred from heaven. His exclusion means that they can no longer be "the accuser of the brothers"[39] before God. The removal of the Church allows him free reign over the earth. He is filled with his own wrath and anger over being cast out. The survivors of Israel and those who receive Christ during the Tribulation become the focus of his anger during the last three and one-half years of his reign.

At the same time, the antichrist receives a mortal wound to the head. He is miraculously healed by the false prophet (Revelation 13:14–15) through Satan's power. The world is deceived into believing that he has come back from the dead and is told to worship him. Apostasy will reign across the world. The "peace treaty" with Israel is broken, and the antichrist takes up his place in the temple, declaring himself to be god. It is "an abomination" (Matthew 24:15) to God and all who are true to the Lord. God's timeline given to Daniel continues to be played out.

At that time Michael shall stand up, The great prince who stands watch over the sons of your people; And there shall be a time of trouble, Such as never was since there was a nation, Even to that time. And at that time your people shall be delivered, Everyone who is found written in the book.
(Daniel 12:1)

He shall speak pompous words against the Most High, Shall persecute the saints of the Most High, And shall intend to change times and law. Then the saints shall be given into his hand For a time and times and half a time.
(Daniel 7:25)

1. Satan and his angels (demonic) are cast out of heaven.
   Luke 10:17–20
2. Lucifer's fall started long ago.
   Ezekiel 28:11–15
   Isaiah 14:12–15
   1 John 3:8
3. Lucifer is the father of lies.
   John 8:42–45

---

39 Zechariah 3:1–5 also tells us about Satan accusing Joshua, the priest.

4. Lucifer's lust for power is his downfall.
   Daniel 8:25
   Daniel 11:36–39
   Revelation 13:4
5. Lucifer and his followers have many times attempted to destroy Jesus.
   Matthew 4:1–3
   Matthew 4:5–6
   Matthew 4:8–9
   John 13:1–2
6. When the antichrist stands in the Holy Place.
   Mark 13:14–20
   Matthew 24:15–22
7. "The Abomination that Makes Desolate" on the earth.
   Daniel 8: 9–14
   Daniel 9:27
   Daniel 11:31–32
8. Many will follow Satan's lies
   2 Thessalonians 2:3–12

The 2,300 Day[40] Historical Prophecy of Daniel 8:14

The future antichrist will in many ways resemble the Greek King of Syria, Antiochus IV Epiphanes, who on September 6, 171 BC conquered and established a reign of terror over the Jewish people. His attention was turned to the destruction of the Jewish culture and national religion. By royal decree he abolished the observance of the Sabbath and all religious festivals. The possession of sacred books and the circumcision of male babies carried the death penalty. As a final act of national humiliation he desecrated the temple by installing an alter to Zeus and began profane animal sacrifices. During his reign he killed tens of thousands of Jews who would not bow to his rule. The persecution spelled out in Daniel 8:14 was prophesized around the year 530 BC, more than 350 years before Antiochus' reign.

The 2,300 days of Daniel 8:14 came to an end in December (Hebrew month of Kislew) of 165 BC, when Jerusalem was retaken by an army of Jews under the leadership of Judas Maccabeus. The days of the prophesy were complete when the temple was cleansed and rededicated near the end of December in 165 BC. At the Feast of Lights, or *Hanukkah,* the Hebrew people reestablished proper worship and sacrifice. The history of these events is also detailed in the Books of Apocrypha, First Maccabees, 1:44–64.

---

40   *The MacArthur Study Bible*, page 1241, commentary on the twenty-three hundred days of Daniel 8:14.

C. The Woman and the Male Child: Revelation. 12:1–6, 12:13–17

(Abomination of Desolation to +1,260, Appendix 4)

> *Now a great sign appeared in heaven: a woman clothed with the sun, with the moon under her feet, and on her head a garland of twelve stars. Then being with child, she cried out in labor and in pain to give birth.*
>
> *Then the woman fled into the wilderness, where she has a place prepared by God, that they should feed her there one thousand two hundred and sixty days.*
>
> *(Revelation 12:1–2, 6)*

Question: What do these Scriptures represent?

John wrote this scripture from the point of view that these events pertain to a future time. It is clear here that they start with the 1,260 days of Great Tribulation (Revelation 12:6). There are three identifiable participants: the Male Child, the Woman, and the Rest of Her Offspring.

The symbolism of the woman clothed with, "the sun, moon, and a garland of twelve stars," has been interpreted to mean the nation Israel and the twelve tribes. I suggest that the Woman is representative of the Messianic Jews, who have become converts to Jesus Christ in the latter days. In Revelation 14:4, the one hundred forty-four thousand of Israel are called, *"the ones who follow the Lamb,"* making their identity clear. In our day, record numbers of Jews are coming to Jesus as the Messiah.

The Woman gives birth. The birth described in Revelation 12:2 is representative of God's plan coming to completion. The true Israel is recognized on that day. The Jews of Israel will look upon Jesus, whom they have pierced, and a remnant will see Him as Messiah. The Woman, believing Israel, is taken into the "wilderness" for protection during the Great Tribulation. She is secured by the blood of Jesus. These events are reminiscent of the great Passover of the death angel during the last plague on Egypt and when Israel escaped from the pursuing Egyptians to the wilderness and Mount Sinai.

1. True Israel is recognized.
   Isaiah 66:7–16
   Ezekiel 39:25–29
2. The Male Child is born.
   Micah 4:6–12
   Micah 5:2–4

3. They will look upon Jesus, whom they have pierced.
   Isaiah 53:4–12
   Zechariah 12:7–10
   Romans 11:25–29
4. A remnant will be saved.
   Zechariah 13:1-2
   Zechariah 13: 8-9

Revelation 12:5 tells us about the Male Child being taken up to heaven. At this time, many of the Hebrew people will now look to heaven and recognize where the true Messiah, *Yeshua*, awaits them. They will, for the first time, recognize Him who was *"taken up"* in the cloud and announced by the angels in Acts 1:9–11.

The Rest of Her Offspring will be persecuted by Satan (Revelation 12:17, 13:7) during the tribulation. I suggest that these are unsaved Jews and other non-Christians, who will come to faith during the time of tribulation and be martyred for their belief.

> *And those of the people who understand shall instruct many; yet for many days they shall fall by sword and flame, by captivity and plundering. Now when they fall, they shall be aided with a little help; but many shall join with them by intrigue. And some of those of understanding shall fall, to refine them, purify them, and make them white, until the time of the end; because it is still for the appointed time.*
>
> *(Daniel 11:33–35)*

D. Great Tribulation Trumpets: Revelation Chapters 8 and 9

(Abomination of Desolation to +1,260, Appendix 4)

> *When He opened the seventh seal, there was silence in heaven for about half an hour. And I saw the seven angels who stand before God, and to them were given seven trumpets.*
> *So the seven angels who had the seven trumpets prepared themselves to sound.*
>
> *(Revelation 8:1-2,6)*

The seals are followed by angels, who carry out judgment through the sounding of trumpets. The sounding trumpets in the Old Testament[41] were

---

[41] Examples: Numbers 10:9–10; 1 Kings 1:34–35; Leviticus 25:8–10.

used for the following purposes: gather the people, assemble the army, proclaim feasts, announce a new king, and declare the Year of Jubilee.

With the breaking of the seventh seal, the Great Tribulation begins. For a time, the heavenly host remains silent. Then God sends forth His trumpets to gather His people, assemble the army of God, to declare judgments and announce the King.

Satan, through the antichrist and the false prophet, continues for this time to have control of religious, political, and economic centers on earth. He continues to lead them with the delusion that he is to be victorious.

1. The altar censer is cast down.
   Revelation 5:8
   Revelation 8:3–5
2. The first four trumpets
   (the great mountain and fallen star destroy the environment).
   a. One-third of green earth destroyed.
      Revelation 8:7
   b. One-third of the seas destroyed.
      Revelation 8:8–9
   c. One-third of the fresh water contaminated.
      Revelation 8:10–11
   d. One-third of the skies darkened.
      Revelation 8:12

Question: What is the significance of the fifth trumpet and the 9:11 angel?

> *And they had as king over them the angel of the bottomless pit, whose name in Hebrew is Abaddon, but in Greek he has the name Apollyon.*
> *(Revelation 9:11)*

In Revelation 9:11, there is a particular angel who is named Apollyon[42] in Greek and Abaddon in Hebrew. Greek mythology played a role in the false gods of the early Church.[43] The names from both the Greek and Hebrew are translated in scripture as "the Destroyer" and literally means "to destroy fully, to perish, or to have no way to flee." In the Old and New Testaments, there are references to "the destroyer" as the instrument of God's judgment. It is suggested that the 9:11 Angel is a fallen angel who torments mankind in the last days. Draw your own conclusions about his significance to current events.

---

42 Apollyon represents worldly forces and the adversary of Christian in John Bunyan's book, "The Pilgrim's Progress".
43 See chapter 5 for the effect of false religion on the early Church.

1. **The First Woe:** The Fifth Trumpet, Revelation 9:11
   a. The "Bottomless Pit" is opened, and the abominations are poured out.
      Revelation 9:2–10
   b. Apollyon or Abaddon, the "Destroyer."
      Old Testament: Exodus 12:23
      New Testament   1 Corinthians 10:7–11
2. **The Second Woe:** The Sixth Trumpet, Revelation 9:12-13
   a. Four angels released, killing one-third of mankind.
      Revelation 9:15
   b. Mankind does not repent.
      Revelation 9:20–21
   c. The 200 million man army formed to fight against Christ.
      Revelation 9:16
      Revelation 16:12–14

E. The Tribulation Harvest: Revelation chapters 7,11 and 14

(to +1,260, Appendix 4)

Early in his ministry, John the Baptist made this prediction:

I indeed baptize you with water unto repentance, but He who is coming after me is mightier than I, whose sandals I am not worthy to carry. He will baptize you with the Holy Spirit and fire. His winnowing fan is in His hand, and He will thoroughly clean out His threshing floor, and gather His wheat into the barn; but He will burn up the chaff with unquenchable fire.

(Matthew 3:11–12)

The Feast of Tabernacles (Ingathering) [44] was held in the fall and reflects the promises of God about the final harvest of the earth. At the end of the age, He will require an accounting of man's stewardship over their lives and His creation. The righteous will be rewarded for their stewardship. The rebellious will be judged and condemned.

He answered and said to them: "He who sows the good seed is the Son of Man. The field is the world, the good seeds are the sons of the kingdom, but the tares are the sons of the wicked one. The enemy who sowed them is the devil, the harvest is the end of the age, and the reapers are the angels. Therefore as the tares are gathered and burned in the fire, so it will be at the end of this age."

(Matthew 13:37-40)

---

44 See chapter 9 and the description of the three harvests.

F. Wheat for the Barn: Revelation 14:1–5, 12–16

(to +1,260, Appendix 4)

The Father's wedding gift to His Son is a harvest and an inheritance. The seeds of the Kingdom were planted at Christ's first advent. The water and fire of the Holy Spirit were given on the day of Pentecost (Acts 2:1), when the Church Age began. The main body of the Church was taken to heaven at the rapture, but there are now others who will be joining their brothers and sisters in heaven. The Tribulation Harvest is ready. Believers are "sealed" by the angels with God's mark of ownership: the Holy Spirit. Jesus will first bring in the wheat, the good crop of the Tribulation.

> *Then He said to His disciples, "The harvest truly is plentiful, but the laborers are few. Therefore pray the Lord of the harvest to send out laborers into His harvest."*
>
> *(Matthew 9:37–38)*

Two of God's witnesses, along with the 144,000 of Israel, are given authority to evangelize and prophesy for 1,260 days of the Great Tribulation. At the end of their ministry, the two witnesses are martyred as the world celebrates their death. After three and a half days, they are resurrected and ascend (*"come up here"*; Revelation 11:12) into heaven in a cloud to the astonishment of their persecutors. Their work on earth is now complete.

Chapter 14 of Revelation begins with Jesus, the Lamb, standing at the gates of heaven, surrounded by the one hundred forty-four thousand witnesses who have been redeemed from the earth. Behind them stands the Host of Heaven, God's angelic army. When the harvest of the wheat is complete, the angelic army awaits God's order to carry out judgment.

1. Witnesses given 1,260 days to testify.
   Revelation 11:2–3
   Revelation 11:7–12
   Revelation 14:1
2. God's protection for 1,260 days given to "overcomers."
   Daniel 12:10
   Zechariah 13:8–9
   Romans 2:5–11

3. "Sealing" by the angel, the righteous spared, the wicked to be punished.
   Ezekiel 9:1–11
   Revelation 7:1–4
   Revelation 9:4
   Revelation 9:20–21
4. *"Blessed are the dead who die in the Lord from now on."*
   Revelation 14:13
5. The "Last Call" before God's wrath is released.
   Joel 2:30–32
   Revelation 18:4
6. Heaven will be "sealed" during God's wrath.
   Revelation 15:8

Then I looked, and behold, a white cloud, and on the cloud sat One like the Son of Man, having on His head a golden crown, and in His hand a sharp sickle. And another angel came out of the temple, crying with a loud voice to Him who sat on the cloud, "Thrust in Your sickle and reap, for the time has come for You to reap, for the harvest of the earth is ripe." So He who sat on the cloud thrust in His sickle on the earth, and the earth was reaped.

(Revelation 14:14–16)

Jesus teaches about the harvest when He tells His disciples the meaning of the parable of the wheat and tares in Matthew chapter 13. An interpretation[45] of Revelation chapter 14, verses 14–16 is that Jesus comes to, *"gather the wheat into my barn"* (Matthew 13:30). It represents the Harvest of the Tribulation saints, the redeemed of Israel, those martyred for their faith, and the *"great multitude"* of believers from the Tribulation (Revelation 14:13). At Daniel's day +1,260, the Tribulation Harvest of the righteous is complete.

Then two men will be in the field: one will be taken and the other left. Two women will be grinding at the mill: one will be taken and the other left. Watch therefore, for you do not know what hour your Lord is coming.

(Matthew 24:40–42)

Matthew chapter 24, verses 36–44, have been a puzzle to many biblical scholars. In these verses, Jesus describes the condition of the world at the time of His Second Coming

---

45   Henry Alford, *The Greek New Testament*, IV, pp. 690–691.

John Walvoord, in his book[46] on prophecy, makes the following statement on this same scripture:

"The time leading up to the Second Coming is compared to the days leading up to the Flood. In both cases there were numerous signs of the approaching end. It should be noted that the signs are in relation to the second coming of Christ at the end of the Tribulation, not to the rapture of the church which has no signs and is imminent until it occurs."

G. The Wine of Wrath and Tares for Burning: Revelation 14:6–11, 17–20

(to +1,260, Appendix 4)

God sends out three final angelic messengers. Even at the last possible moment during the Tribulation, God's provision of salvation is announced to those who have refused to receive His grace. They are without excuse. Heaven will no longer wait, and the final act occurs when God pours out his wrath.

Then I saw another angel flying in the midst of heaven, having the everlasting gospel to preach to those who dwell on the earth—to every nation, tribe, tongue, and people saying with a loud voice, "Fear God and give glory to Him, for the hour of His judgment has come; and worship Him who made heaven and earth, the sea and springs of water."

(Revelation 14:6–7)

1. The three angelic Messengers
   Messenger of the Gospel   Revelation 14:6–7
   Messenger of the bad news   Revelation 14:8
   Messenger of condemnation   Revelation 14:9–11

Then another angel came out of the temple which is in heaven, he also having a sharp sickle.

And another angel came out from the altar, who had power over fire, and he cried with a loud cry to him who had the sharp sickle, saying, "Thrust in your sharp sickle and gather the clusters of the vine of the earth, for her grapes are fully ripe." So the angel thrust his sickle into the earth and gathered the vine of the earth, and threw it into the great winepress of the wrath of God. And the winepress was trampled outside the city, and blood came out of the winepress, up to the horses' bridles, for one thousand six hundred furlongs.

(Revelation 14:17–20)

---

46 John Walvoord, *The Prophecy Knowledge Handbook*, 1990, p. 392.

2. The Wrath of God begins.
   Deuteronomy 32:35
   Romans 12:19
   Revelation 6:17
   Revelation 14:17–20

H. The Wrath of God: Revelation Chapter 15 through 16:16

(+1,261 to +1,289, Appendix 4)

Then I saw another sign in heaven, great and marvelous: seven angels having the seven last plagues, for in them the wrath of God is complete.

(Revelation15:1)

Then I heard a loud voice from the temple saying to the seven angels, "Go and pour out the bowls of the wrath of God on the earth."

(Revelation 16:1)

The harvest of the righteous will be complete before the sounding of the Seventh Trumpet. All of those under, "the shadow of the Almighty," have come home and into His House. The doors of heaven are sealed so that no one else can enter. When the Seventh Trumpet sounds, the first of the Seven Bowls of the Wrath of God are poured out. In keeping with Daniel's timeline, I believe these events occur after day 1,260 and before day 1,290. There will be no escape from God's wrath.

Come, my people, enter your chambers, And shut your doors behind you; Hide yourself, as it were, for a little moment, Until the indignation is past. For behold, the L ORD *comes out of His place To punish the inhabitants of the earth for their iniquity; The earth will also disclose her blood, And will no more cover her slain. In that day the* L ORD *with His severe sword, great and strong, will punish Leviathan the fleeing serpent, Leviathan that twisted serpent; And He will slay the reptile that is in the sea.*

(Isaiah 26:20–27:1)

Just like Pharaoh's refusal of God at the hand of Moses to release His people, the world refuses to yield to the Lord. The final plague of the death angel came to judge Egypt. I believe that the Day of the Lord and the Seventh Bowl of God's Wrath describe a similar event.

1. God's final indictment: Fallen man has killed the prophets and saints of God.
   Psalm 94:3–7
   Revelation 18:20
   Revelation 18:24
2. **The Third Woe:** The Seventh Trumpet, Revelation 11:14
   a. The Kingdoms are to be delivered.
      Revelation 11:15
   b. God asserts His Reign over the earth
      Revelation 11:16-17
   c. Anger of the nations towards God.
      Revelation 11:18
   d. The Last Seven Plagues.
      Revelation 15:1, 5–7
   e. The Song of Moses and the Song of the Lamb.
      Exodus 15:1–19
      Revelation 15:2–4

O Lord God, to whom vengeance belongs—O God, to whom vengeance belongs, shine forth! Rise up, O Judge of the earth; Render punishment to the proud. Lord , how long will the wicked, How long will the wicked triumph?

(Psalm 94:1-3)

In Revelation chapter 16, the Wrath of God begins. The plagues are for Satan, the false prophet, the false church, the antichrist, the demonic followers, and those who follow in their rebellion against God. The "Harlot" is the symbol for the three forces of a false religion, political power, and economic seduction that exist on earth during the time of the Tribulation.

See that you do not refuse Him who speaks. For if they did not escape who refused Him who spoke on earth, much more shall we not escape if we turn away from Him who speaks from heaven, whose voice then shook the earth; but now He has promised, saying, "Yet once more I shake not only the earth, but also heaven." Now this, "Yet once more," indicates the removal of those things that are being shaken, as of things that are made, that the things which cannot be shaken may remain.

Therefore, since we are receiving a kingdom which cannot be shaken, let us have grace, by which we may serve God acceptably with reverence and godly fear. For our God is a consuming fire.

(Hebrews 12:25–29)

1. God is Righteous to Judge.
   Romans 1:18–21
   Revelation 16:5–7
2. The First Six Bowls (plagues) of God's Judgment.
   a. The plague of sores.
      Revelation 16:2
   b. The plague on the sea.
      Revelation 16:3
   c. The plague on the rivers.
      Revelation 16:4
   d. The plague from the sun.
      Revelation 16:8–9
   e. The plague on Satan's seat of power.
      Revelation 16:10–11
   f. The plague for Satan's army.
      Revelation 16:12–14

I. The Day of the Lord: Revelation 16:15 through 18:24, 19:11–16

(Day +1,290, Appendix 4)

The armies of Satan will have surrounded the city of Jerusalem. The main body of their army will be on the plains of Megiddo. It is a place where great wars have already occurred. Satan's final attempt is to hold the Holy Ground around Jerusalem and, thereby, thwart the return of Christ.

And they gathered them together to the place called in Hebrew, Megiddo.

Then the seventh angel poured out his bowl into the air, and a loud voice came out of the temple of heaven, from the throne, saying, "It is done!"

(Revelation 16:16–17)

In Revelation chapter 19, we see Jesus mounted upon a white horse, ready to enter the final battle. He takes His rightful place as *"King of Kings and Lord of Lords"* over all the earth. In this final battle, Jesus defeats Satan and asserts His reign. *"The Kingdom of Heaven is at Hand."* The battle that will ensue will be worldwide and not just limited to Jerusalem and the plains of Megiddo.

Now I saw heaven opened, and behold, a white horse. And He who sat on him was called Faithful and True, and in righteousness He judges and makes war. His eyes were like a flame of fire, and on His head were many crowns. He had a name written that no one knew except Himself.

> *He was clothed with a robe dipped in blood, and His name is called The Word of God. And the armies in heaven, clothed in fine linen, white and clean, followed Him on white horses. Now out of His mouth goes a sharp sword, that with it He should strike the nations. And He Himself will rule them with a rod of iron. He Himself treads the winepress of the fierceness and wrath of Almighty God. And He has on His robe and on His thigh a name written:*
> KING OF KINGS AND LORD OF LORDS.
> *(Revelation 19:11–16)*

The phrase, *"the Day of the Lord"*[47] appears nineteen times in the Old Testament and four times in the New Testament. The world domination of the antichrist, which began with the peace agreement with the Jews and the setting up of the abomination of desolation in the Holy City lasts until day 1,290 (Daniel 12:11). The Day of the Lord will occur in a single day, not unlike the time when the ancient kingdom of Babylon was captured by the Medes and Persians in Daniel 5:22–30. It fits Daniel's timeline for Day 1,290, as it brings to an end Satan's control and the antichrist's reign.

> *When you see this, your heart shall rejoice, And your bones shall flourish like grass; The hand of the LORD shall be known to His servants, And His indignation to His enemies. For behold, the LORD will come with fire And with His chariots, like a whirlwind, To render His anger with fury, And His rebuke with flames of fire. For by fire and by His sword The LORD will judge all flesh; And the slain of the LORD shall be many.*
> *(Isaiah 66:14–16)*

1. "It is done": The Day of the Lord arrives.
   Revelation 16:17–21
2. Judgment of the false religious systems.
   Revelation 17:1–9
3. Judgment of the world's political systems.
   Revelation 17:10–18
4. Judgment of the world's economic systems.
   Revelation 18:1–24

When Jesus sets His feet down on the Mount of Olives, a great earthquake splits and enlarges the valley between it and the city of Jerusalem. The landscape of the country is forever changed. The final battle ensues, and Jesus is victorious.

---

47 See the *John MacArthur Study Bible* footnote on Isaiah 2:12, p. 958, for a complete list.

And there were noises and thunderings and lightnings; and there was a great earthquake, such a mighty and great earthquake as had not occurred since men were on the earth. ⁹Now the great city was divided into three parts, and the cities of the nations fell. And great Babylon was remembered before God, to give her the cup of the wine of the fierceness of His wrath.

(Revelation 16:18–19)

Then the Lord will go forth, And fight against those nations, As He fights in the day of battle. And in that day His feet will stand on the Mount of Olives, Which faces Jerusalem on the east. And the Mount of Olives shall be split in two, From east to west, Making a very large valley; Half of the mountain shall move toward the north And half of it toward the south.

(Zechariah 14:3–4)

1. Jesus leads the Armies (Host) of Heaven in battle at Megiddo.
   Malachi 4:1–6
   Matthew 24:29–31
   Isaiah 66:14–16
2. Christ's arrival from Glory to the Mount of Olives.
   Luke 21:25–28
3. The battle (Day of Darkness) will be all in one day.
   Zechariah 14:5–7
   Zechariah 14:12–15
   Joel 2:10–11
   Revelation 18:8
   Revelation 18:19–20
4. Satan and his followers are bound by Jesus for one thousand years.
   Isaiah 24:21–22
   Jude 6, 14–15
   Revelation 20:1–3

Who is this who comes from Edom, With dyed garments from Bozrah, This One who is glorious in His apparel, Traveling in the greatness of His strength?—"I who speak in righteousness, mighty to save." Why is Your apparel red, And Your garments like one who treads in the winepress? I have trodden the winepress alone, And from the peoples no one was with Me. For I have trodden them in My anger, And trampled them in My fury; Their blood is sprinkled upon My garments, And I have stained all My robes. For the day of vengeance is in My heart, And the year of My redeemed has come. I looked, but there was no one to help, And

I wondered that there was no one to uphold; Therefore My own arm brought salvation for Me; And My own fury, it sustained Me.
(Isaiah 63:1–5)

J. The Earth Is "Cleansed": Revelation 19:17 through 20:3
(Day +1,291 to +1,334, Appendix 4)

Jesus completes the final requirement in the New (Marriage) Covenant. The nation of Israel will be established, and the city of Jerusalem will be the center of Christ's reign on earth. The antichrist and the false prophet are cast into hell and the lake of fire. Satan is bound until the end of Christ's millennial reign.

And unless those days were shortened, no flesh would be saved; but for the elect's sake those days will be shortened.
(Matthew 24:22)

Even with the completion of the wrath of God and the Day of the Lord, there are lives that are spared. The survivors are to enter into the millennium. There are non-messianic Jews and Israelites among the survivors.

1. The Survivors List (Old Testament).
   Isaiah 1:9
   Isaiah 10:20-22
   Joel 3:1–3
2. The Survivors List (New Testament).
   Romans 9: 27–29
   Matthew 13:40–43
   Matthew 13:47–50
   Matthew 24:22
   1 Thessalonians 1:6-10

Jesus returns to heaven and proclaims victory. The inheritance has been secured. The final elements of God's promises to the Bride of Christ have been put in place. The final cleansing of earth takes place during the marriage ceremony of the Lamb and His Bride. It is also before the start of Christ's millennial reign. All things that are an abomination to God will be cleansed. The dead bodies that have lain on the battlefield and in the streets will be removed. The earth will undergo a transformation, being made ready for Christ's reign.

1. The antichrist and the false prophet receive divine punishment.
   Isaiah 34:8–10
   Revelation 14:9–11
   Revelation 19:20
2. The nations who followed Satan will be cleansed.
   Matthew 25:31–33
3. False prophets and the false religions will be cleansed.
   Ezekiel 13:8–9
   Isaiah 2:5–12
   Zephaniah 1:2–7
4. The world's false economic system (greed and lust for power) is cleansed.
   1 Timothy 6:1–11
   1 Timothy 6:17
   Revelation 18:9–19
5. The "Great Supper" and the invasion of birds.
   Ezekiel 39:17–20
   Revelation 19:17–21

Jesus Publically Claims His Bride: Revelation 19:1–8

(*Day +1,291 to +1,334, Appendix 4*)

The ceremony of Christ and His beloved Bride takes place in the presence of the Father and is witnessed by the heavenly host. All of the provisions of God's inheritance are fully secured. The second cup of the New Covenant (Blood Covenant Promise),[48] which Jesus promised in Matthew 26:28–29, is ready to be taken, finalizing the Marriage Covenant. The promises made in the covenant have been authenticated by the Father. The final events of the seclusion, or *yichud*, and the Marriage Supper of the Lamb will soon take place. Christ has kept His Word. Heaven celebrates!

> *And I heard, as it were, the voice of a great multitude, as the sound of many waters and as the sound of mighty thunderings, saying, "Alleluia! For the Lord God Omnipotent reigns! Let us be glad and rejoice and give Him glory, for the marriage of the Lamb has come, and His wife has made herself ready. And to her it was granted to be arrayed in fine linen, clean and bright, for the fine linen is the righteous acts of the saints."*
>
> (*Revelation 19:6–8*)

---

[48] See chapter 8 on the Marriage Covenant.

Oh, give thanks to the LORD, for He is good! For His mercy endures forever. Let the redeemed of the LORD say so, Whom He has redeemed from the hand of the enemy, And gathered out of the lands, From the east and from the west, From the north and from the south.

(Psalm 107:1–3)

The bride receives a new name, signifying the change of identity. At this point, the Church moves from being the Betrothed Bride of Christ to being seated at His side.

To the faithful of Israel:
You shall no longer be termed Forsaken, Nor shall your land any more be termed Desolate; But you shall be called Hephzibah, and your land Beulah; For the LORD delights in you, And your land shall be married. For as a young man marries a virgin, So shall your sons marry you; And as the bridegroom rejoices over the bride, So shall your God rejoice over you.

(Isaiah 62:4–5)

To the faithful of the Church:
He who has an ear, let him hear what the Spirit says to the churches. To him who overcomes I will give some of the hidden manna to eat. And I will give him a white stone, and on the stone a new name written which no one knows except him who receives it.

(Revelation 2:17)

The Angel with *"The Little Book"*: Revelation Chapter 10

But in the days of the sounding of the seventh angel, when he is about to sound, the mystery of God would be finished, as He declared to His servants the prophets.

Then the voice which I heard from heaven spoke to me again and said, "Go, take the little book which is open in the hand of the angel who stands on the sea and on the earth."

So I went to the angel and said to him, "Give me the little book." Then I took the little book out of the angel's hand and ate it, and it was as sweet as honey in my mouth. But when I had eaten it, my stomach became bitter. And he said to me, "You must prophesy again about many peoples, nations, tongues, and kings."

(Revelation 10:7–11)

The angel completes his message to John, and he delivers the "Little Book" into John's hands. In Revelation, Jesus completes the prophetic word He started with the Olivet Discourse.

Matthew Henry says, "I have tasted in it (God's Word) that the Lord is gracious; and the most subtle disputant cannot convince one who has tasted honey that it is not sweet."[49] To the Apostle John, it is sweet to be given the Revelation of Jesus. But, with the Word comes the responsibility of being the prophet who is to deliver a message of judgment and tribulation. John is told to consume the book, and in so doing, he becomes the messenger of God to, *"many peoples, nations, tongues, and kings."* It is not an easy message to deliver, but it is an important message of God's plan of redemption.

1. Sweet Words given to Prophets.
   Ezekiel 3:1–4
   Jeremiah 15:16

In John's proclamation of the book of Revelation, the mystery of God's plan is "finished." The final chapter has been written over the rebellion of Satan and man. Sin will no longer reign on earth. Christ's throne is established. He is "LORD OF LORDS AND KING OF KINGS."

Believers in Christ are to encourage and strengthen each other, as we see these days approaching. We need to remember the ending of the prophecy and its message of "Good News" for the believer. Words of encouragement are written throughout the Old and New Testaments. The book of Revelation ends God's plan with the Marriage Supper of the Lamb, the millennial reign of Christ, and the New Heaven and New Earth. Hidden behind the pages of tribulation and judgment is God's great love for a people to call His own.

> *Let us hold fast the confession of our hope without wavering, for He who promised is faithful. And let us consider one another in order to stir up love and good works, not forsaking the assembling of ourselves together, as is the manner of some, but exhorting one another, and so much the more as you see the Day approaching.*
> *(Hebrews 10:23–25)*

---

[49] Matthew Henrys Commentary on the NT, Preface to Volume 5, Parson's Technology Inc. copyright1998

Chapter 13
Yichud, The Seclusion

> ### Yichud, the Seclusion
> At the end of the ceremony, the bride and groom go into the actual Chuppah or wedding chamber for a time of seclusion called *yichud*. The *yichud* precedes the *seudas mitzvah*, or marriage supper. Up to this point, the bride- to-be has worn her hair in the up position or has covered her head. Now, she undoes her hair and lets it hang loosely, indicating her submission to her husband. The door to the wedding chamber is closed and locked from the inside. The groom's friend, or witness, stands guard outside.
>
> There is no more beautiful earthly picture than that of the relationship of a man and his wife whose most heartfelt desires are to establish each other in their relationship. It is in the *yichud* that their relationship is made complete.

The Seclusion: Revelation 21:9–22:6
(Day +1,291 to Day +1,334 Appendix 4)

In keeping with the wedding tradition, the seclusion in heaven of the Bride of Christ will occur after the Day of the Lord and before the wedding supper. All who are to participate in the wedding have been assembled in the tabernacle of heaven. The Bride, the Church, is to undergo a final transformation. God's love story unfolds.

> *One thing I have desired of the LORD, That will I seek: That I may dwell in the house of the LORD All the days of my life, To behold the beauty of the LORD, And to inquire in His temple. For in the time of trouble He shall hide me in His pavilion; In the secret place of His*

tabernacle He shall hide me; He shall set me high upon a rock And now my head shall be lifted up above my enemies all around me; Therefore I will offer sacrifices of joy in His tabernacle; I will sing, yes, I will sing praises to the LORD.

(Psalm 27:4–6)

"For your Maker is your husband, The LORD of hosts is His name; And your Redeemer is the Holy One of Israel; He is called the God of the whole earth. For the LORD has called you like a woman forsaken and grieved in spirit, Like a youthful wife when you were refused," Says your God. "For a mere moment I have forsaken you, But with great mercies I will gather you. With a little wrath I hid My face from you for a moment; But with everlasting kindness I will have mercy on you," Says the LORD, your Redeemer.

(Isaiah 54:5–8)

I believe that the *chuppah* represents the New Jerusalem as pictured in Revelation chapter 21. It is a place of beauty beyond measure. The wonders are the handiwork of Christ that He has been preparing for nearly two thousand years. At the time of the *yichud*, this marvelous abode remains in heaven. It will also remain in heaven during the one thousand–year reign of Christ on earth but will be joined to the earth when God makes the New Heaven and New Earth. The glories described give us insight into the nature of the *chuppah*.

But I saw no temple in it, for the Lord God Almighty and the Lamb are its temple. The city had no need of the sun or of the moon to shine in it, for the glory of God illuminated it. The Lamb is its light.

(Revelation 21:22–23)

Christ and His Bride will be inside this chamber, as He is preparing her to be ready to rule and reign with Him. The Bride will be remade in the likeness of Christ, without a sin nature, and will live with Him forever.

Blessed are the pure in heart, For they shall see God.

(Matthew 5:8)

The Church will be placed in a position of authority under His reign over the earth. Christ's desire is our fulfillment in Him, the sharing in His glory, and to reign at His side.

> *To him who overcomes I will grant to sit with Me on My throne, as I also overcame and sat down with My Father on His throne.*
> *(Revelation 3:21)*

The book of Daniel and the book of Hebrews tell us about the refining and purification process that will happen during the seclusion.

> *Many shall be purified, made white, and refined, but the wicked shall do wickedly; and none of the wicked shall understand, but the wise shall understand.*
> *(Daniel 12:10)*

> *But you have come to Mount Zion and to the city of the living God, the heavenly Jerusalem, to an innumerable company of angels, to the general assembly and church of the firstborn who are registered in heaven, to God the Judge of all, to the spirits of just men made perfect, to Jesus the Mediator of the new covenant.*
> *(Hebrews 12:22–24a)*

1. The Bride is transformed.
   Psalm 51:1–2, 7–11
   Titus 2:11–14
2. Lives that reflect His Glory.
   2 Corinthians 4:6–7
   2 Peter 1:16–19
3. Allowed to enter His courts.
   Psalm 65:4
   Psalm 100:1–5
4. Rejoicing in His presence.
   Psalm 84:1–4
   Psalm 95:1–3
5. The "Mystery" that was secret is now revealed.
   Ephesians 5:29–32
   Matthew 13:11–17
   1 Corinthians 2:7–10

What began as the work of the Holy Spirit during the Church age will be made complete during the *yichud*. When we were under the tutelage of the Holy Spirit, believers are seen as being in positional perfection; that is, they are seen through the blood of Christ. He has loved us even through our imperfections. Now, the process of glorification is to be made complete. Here, the Church will be transformed into His image and likeness. "*We shall see Him as He is.*" His glory and love will shine through our lives and our eyes.

> *Behold what manner of love the Father has bestowed on us, that we should be called children of God! Therefore the world does not know us, because it did not know Him. Beloved, now we are children of God; and it has not yet been revealed what we shall be, but we know that when He is revealed, we shall be like Him, for we shall see Him as He is. And everyone who has this hope in Him purifies himself, just as He is pure.*
> *(1 John 3:1–3)*

Chapter 14
Seudas Mitzvah, The Marriage Supper

Seudas Mitzvah, the Marriage Supper

The Marriage Supper is held at the end of the yichud. When it is time for the couple to appear, the groom signals to his witness by knocking on the door from the inside. The witness then announces and introduces the couple as the groom opens the door, exits the *chuppah*, and appears with his bride before the assembled guests.

At the wedding supper, there are four groups of people: (1) the Bride and Groom, (2) their families, (3) the attendants of the bride and groom, and (4) the invited guests.

The guests participate in the *seudas mitzvah*, or *L'Sameach Choson v' Kallah*, to celebrate in joy for the new couple as they start their married life. They celebrate by dancing around the couple as an expression of support. At the end of the meal and celebration, the second blessing, or *brachot,* is repeated by the rabbi.

John Cooper

The Marriage Supper: Revelation 19:9–10

(*Day +1,291 to Day +1,334, Appendix 4*)

> ***Blessed are those who are called to the marriage supper of The Lamb!***[50]
>
> Then he said to me, "Write: "Blessed are those who are called to the marriage supper of the Lamb!" And he said to me, "These are the true sayings of God."
>
> (*Revelation 19:9*)

Some have placed the *seudas mitzvah* of the Lamb shortly after the rapture. In the Hebrew wedding, it was customary to save the best part of the celebration until last. I would suggest that the celebration be placed near the end of Daniel's time frame, between days 1,290 and 1,335.

Christ and the Church appear after the seclusion. The glory that surrounds Jesus is greater than a glorious sunrise. His glory fills the heavenly city. The symbolism of Revelation chapter 21 is that the Bride and the city (New Jerusalem) are one and the same. The city is God's chosen people, and God's Glory shines and is reflected throughout the city.

> *The heavens declare the glory of God; And the firmament shows His handiwork … Their line has gone out through all the earth, And their words to the end of the world. In them He has set a tabernacle for the sun, Which is like a bridegroom coming out of his chamber, And rejoices like a strong man to run its race.*
>
> (*Psalm 19:1, 4–5*)

> *Come, I will show you the bride, the Lamb's wife. And he carried me away in the Spirit to a great and high mountain, and showed me the great city, the holy Jerusalem, descending out of heaven from God, having the glory of God. Her light was like a most precious stone, like a jasper stone, clear as crystal.*
>
> (*Revelation 21:9b–11*)

> *I will greatly rejoice in the* LORD, *My soul shall be joyful in my God; For He has clothed me with the garments of salvation, He has covered me with the robe of righteousness, As a bridegroom decks himself with ornaments, And as a bride adorns herself with her jewels.*
>
> (*Isaiah 61:10*)

---

50   The fourth of seven blessings listed in Revelation. See appendix 1.

The angels and the Host of heaven rejoice and celebrate. Those who overcame and were victorious during the Tribulation are recognized. The marriage supper represents God's plan to bless a chosen people. Being invited to the marriage supper of the Lamb is God's love for mankind expressed in its highest form. Through His grace, He showers upon us what we did not earn or deserve. His nature is love.

Question: Who will attend the marriage supper?

1. Those who are called/invited.
   Matthew 22:2–14
   Luke 14:16-24
2. Those saved before Pentecost.
   Hebrews 11:13–16
3. Tribulation saints.
   Revelation 7:13–17
4. Martyrs of the tribulation.
   Revelation 6:9–11
5. The redeemed multitude of tribulation.
   Revelation 7:9–10
6. The one hundred forty-four thousand redeemed of Israel.
   Revelation 7:4–8
   Revelation 14:3–4
7. Those in the Book of Life.
   Luke 10:20
   Revelation 3:5

For a day in Your courts is better than a thousand. I would rather be a doorkeeper in the house of my God Than dwell in the tents of wickedness. For the LORD God is a sun and shield; The LORD will give grace and glory; No good thing will He withhold From those who walk uprightly. O LORD of hosts, Blessed is the man who trusts in You!
(Psalm 84:10–12)

Ho! Everyone who thirsts, Come to the waters; And you who have no money, Come, buy and eat. Yes, come, buy wine and milk Without money and without price. Why do you spend money for what is not bread, And your wages for what does not satisfy? Listen carefully to Me, and eat what is good, And let your soul delight itself in abundance.
(Isaiah 55:1–2)

Chapter 15

Millennial Reign of Christ

The Millennial Reign of Christ

The groom and his bride begin their life together at his father's village. The additional rooms the groom prepared during the betrothal is their new home. Their marriage relationship is a three-way covenant between the husband, the wife, and God. Each assumes their God-directed role in the marriage, as they fulfill their purpose to love, cherish, and honor each other. Children arrive. The children are instructed in the faith, as the couple continues to grow in their own relationship with God. Reading and following the instructions from the Torah are a part of their daily lives. Hebrew rituals and days of celebration are observed to affirm their call to be followers of Jehovah God. There is fulfillment and joy in following God.

Earth is brought into subjection to Christ[51]: Revelation 20:1–6

(+1,000 years, Appendix 4)

> *Then Jesus came and spoke to them saying, "All authority has been given to Me in heaven and on earth."*
>
> (Matthew 28:18)

> *Then comes the end, when He (Christ) delivers the kingdom to God the Father, when He puts an end to all rule and authority and power. For He (Christ) must reign till He has put all enemies under His feet. The last enemy that will be destroyed is death. For "He has put all things under His feet." But when He says "all things are put under* Him*," it is evident that He who put all things under Him is excepted. Now when all things are made subject to Him, then the Son Himself will also be subject to Him (the Father) who put all things under Him that God may be all in all.*
>
> *(1 Corinthians 15:24–28)*

The Millennial Kingdom is the final stage in the process re-creation of the earth prior to the Father's coming from His throne to establish the New Heaven and New Earth.

Christ rules with a *"rod of iron"* (Revelation 19:15) during the thousand-year reign. The curse, with its lies, destruction, and death, will be subject to Him. The order of the old things will be turned upside down, and the new order will be found in the teaching that flows from His throne in Jerusalem.

Christ will reign until He has put all enemies under His feet. During the reign, sin and death will continue to have a hold because of those who continue to rebel.

When the last barriers are removed, Christ will take the realm of earth and return its dominion back to the Father. The stages of change during the Millennium:

    A. Jesus reigns!
    B. Resurrected believers will serve at His side.
    C. The curse is removed.
    D. Jerusalem, the seat of worship and government.
    E. Israel and Judah restored for service in Jerusalem.
    F. The Sabbath and Millennial feasts will be observed.
    G. The Great White Throne judgment.

---

51   Lori Weaks, from the class on *The Groom's Arrival* at Shiloh Church, is to be credited with directing me to her insight of I Corinthians 15:24–28.

A. Jesus Reigns! Revelation 20:1–6

(Day +1,335, Appendix 4)

And they lived and reigned with Christ for a thousand years.
(Revelation 20:4c)

Blessed is he who waits, and comes to the one thousand three hundred and thirty-five days. "But you, go your way till the end; for you shall rest, and will arise to your inheritance at the end of the days."
(Daniel 12:12–13)

Repent therefore and be converted, that your sins may be blotted out, so that times of refreshing may come from the presence of the Lord, and that He may send Jesus Christ, who was preached to you before, whom heaven must receive until the times of restoration of all things, which God has spoken by the mouth of all His holy prophets since the world began.
(Acts 3:19–21)

Christ's thousand-year millennial reign on earth begins on Daniel's day 1,335.

The One who ascended into heaven (Acts 1:9) and has been seated at the Father's right hand returns to earth in His resurrected body. The King of the tribe of David will sit in the halls of Jerusalem, leading His people and directing the affairs of mankind. This time, He is recognized by the Hebrew people who rejected Him at His first advent. He will be their king and He will reign with justice.

With the Church's marriage to Christ, the grace and beauty of God's plan will have only just begun. The "Blessed" hope and truth of the Christian faith is in the marriage of the Lamb of God to His people. It is only the beginning of something wonderful! These changes will continue to grow and transform His Bride for time eternal. The continuous revelation of God's inheritance and blessings will become the hallmark of His creation.

I was watching in the night visions, And behold, One like the Son of Man, Coming with the clouds of heaven! He came to the Ancient of Days, And they brought Him near before Him. Then to Him was given dominion and glory and a kingdom, That all peoples, nations, and languages should serve Him. His dominion is an everlasting dominion,

Which shall not pass away, And His kingdom the one Which shall not be destroyed.

(Daniel 7:13–14)

1. All authority on earth belongs to Christ.
   Daniel 2:44
   Jeremiah 33:15–18
2. He will bring in a just reign.
   Isaiah 2:4
   Isaiah 11:1–5
   Jeremiah 33:15–18
   Psalm 72:1–4
3. All nations will serve Him.
   Psalm 2:7–12
   Isaiah 60:3–5
   1 Timothy 6:13-15
4. The nations will be blessed.
   Micah 4:1–5
   Isaiah 12:4–6
   Matthew 25:34–40
5. His Glory will fill the earth.
   Isaiah 60:19–20
   Titus 2:13
   1 Timothy 6: 16

B. Resurrected Believers Will Serve at His Side: Revelation 20:4–6

(+1,000 years, Appendix 4)

Blessed is he who has a part in the first resurrection[52]

But the rest of the dead did not live again until the thousand years were finished. This is the first resurrection. Blessed and holy is he who has part in the first resurrection. Over such the second death has no power, but they shall be priests of God and of Christ, and shall reign with Him a thousand years.

(Revelation 20:5–6)

---

52 The fifth of seven blessings listed in Revelation. See appendix 1.

Question: What is the first resurrection?

Jesus was the firstfruit of the resurrection from earth. At Jesus' return (n*isuin*) for His Bride, the Church becomes the first of God's harvest of earth. Christ is the steward of the renewed creation. God's people receive their resurrected physical bodies for the purpose of reestablishing God's plan on earth. The Church, the Bride of Christ, will be stewards with Him in His reign. The Church's preparation will have been completed during the *yichud* and the events that took place in heaven during the wedding celebration. What was created and lost due to sin will ultimately be returned to God's dominion in its fully restored form.

Each member of the Bride of the Lamb will have a role in bringing tribulation survivors under Christ's new order. Needs will be met. Hearts will change. Wounds will be healed. They will learn to *"war no more."* Differences in the operation of nations and economies will be resolved through the loving care and compassion of Christ's representatives. Mankind's search for happiness and peace will be fulfilled during the Millennium. Even under these conditions, a part of humanity will still choose to live in rebellion and a fallen state.

1. The inheritance of the saints has been preserved.
   Matthew 25:23
   Ephesians 2:4–7
   1 Peter 1:3–5
2. The redeemed will serve as stewards of His Kingdom.
   1 Corinthians 6:2–3
   Revelation 1:5–6
   Revelation 2:26–27
   Revelation 3:21

C. The Curse Is Removed

God's plan has always been to bless man and to bless His creation. The curse began when Adam and Eve sinned. There was an immediate "death" upon their separation from God. Adam and Eve were cast out of Paradise, and their access was blocked by an angel with a "flaming sword" (Genesis 3:24). The curse that followed them included the earth and the environment (Genesis 3:17–18). Living would be earned by hard work (Genesis 3:19). Life would be perpetuated through the pain of birth (Genesis 3:16).

With Christ's return, the grip of Satan's dominion over the realm of earth has been broken. The Millennial Reign brings about steps of restoration. The old Paradise order that was in Eden will begin to return. The Millennium will be marked by a universal peace. The transformation will be complete at the end of the Millennium, when we will see the New Heaven and the New Earth.

The Curse

1. Adam's sin and the curse.
   Genesis 3:17–19
   Romans 8:19–22
2. The curse of death.
   Genesis 3:3
   1 Corinthians 15:54–56
   Romans 6:22–23
3. The curse of living under the "Law" versus living under grace.
   Deuteronomy 27:26
   Romans 3:19–23
   Galatians 3:10–14
4. The present world's operating system.
   John 15:18–19
   John 16:33
   Ephesians 2:2–3

The Post-Curse World

5. The curse is removed.
   John 12:31–32
   John 16:8–11
   Isaiah 35:1–7
   Isaiah 55:12–13
   Isaiah 65:25
6. Universal peace.
   Isaiah 2:2–4
   Isaiah 11:6–12
   Isaiah 65:23
7. Human life span and death.
   Isaiah 65:20
   Psalm 92:12–15
8. Human activity.
   Isaiah 65:21-22
   Jeremiah 32:42–44
   Jeremiah 33:7–9

9. Access to God.
   Isaiah 56:6–8
   Isaiah 65:24
   Zechariah 14:16
10. Stewards of God's Commandments.
    Matthew 20:25–28
    Matthew 22:36–40
    John 13:34–35

D. Jerusalem: The Seat of Worship and Government

And in that day it shall be That living waters shall flow from Jerusalem, Half of them toward the eastern sea And half of them toward the western sea; In both summer and winter it shall occur. And the LORD shall be King over all the earth. In that day it shall be—"The LORD is one," And His name one. All the land shall be turned into a plain from Geba to Rimmon south of Jerusalem. Jerusalem shall be raised up and inhabited in her place from Benjamin's Gate to the place of the First Gate and the Corner Gate, and from the Tower of Hananel to the king's winepresses. The people shall dwell in it; And no longer shall there be utter destruction, But Jerusalem shall be safely inhabited.
(Zechariah 14:8–11)

For the LORD shall build up Zion; He shall appear in His glory.
(Psalm 102:16)

The great earthquake that occurs when Jesus arrives on the Mount of Olives (Zechariah 14:4) alters the topography of the city of Jerusalem. The city prepares to be the seat of worship and government during Christ's Millennial Reign.

The Holy City and the temple mount are again filled with the *shekinah* glory. The Millennial Temple (Ezekiel 40–48) will stand on the temple mount, and the nations will come before the Lord. Jesus Himself will be our Lord and rightful high priest. God's blessings and presence will once again be with His people.

1. Christ returns, full of Glory.
   Matthew 16:27–28
   John 17:4–5
   Psalm 24:7–10
   Psalm 145:5–12
   Revelation 5:13

2. The Glory once departed (Ichabod), returns.
   Ezekiel 10:18–19
   Ezekiel 11:22–23
   Ezekiel 43:1–9
3. What mankind is looking for: "The City."
   Zechariah 8:3–6
   Philippians 3:20–21
   Hebrews 11:14–16
4. The Tabernacle of Meeting.
   Exodus 29:43–46
   Isaiah 4:2–6
   2 Corinthians 6:16
5. The Millennial Temple.
   Ezekiel 45:1–5
   Haggai 2:6–9

E. Israel and Judah Restored for Service in Jerusalem *(See Appendix 2)*

The last anointed King over all of Israel was Solomon (921 BC). In 721 BC, Israel (ten northern tribes) was conquered by Assyria (2 Kings 16:1–17:41) and dispersed among foreign nations. Some modern Jews hold to the belief that only the *Meshach* (Messiah) will be the one to bring back the ten lost tribes to rejoin the Jews at the time of His appearance. The rejoined representatives of Judah and Israel who have come to *Yeshua* as Messiah will serve in the restored city and sanctuary. At Christ's first advent, the Hebrew people were given a Lamb for redemption rather than a King. He now comes, and the survivors of Israel see Him not only as their Lamb but as their rightful King.

The nations that have persecuted Israel for thousands of years will now hold them in a place of honor. The disputes over the Holy Land will have come to an end. Jerusalem will be a city for all mankind, a city of wonder and peace, ruled by the Prince of Peace.

David my servant shall be king over them, and they shall have one shepherd; they shall also walk in My judgments and observe My statues, and do them. Then they shall dwell in the land that I have given to Jacob My servant, where your fathers dwelt; and they shall dwell there, they, their children, and their children's children, forevermore; and My servant David shall be their prince forever. Moreover I will make a covenant of peace with them, and it shall be an everlasting covenant with them; I will establish them and multiply them, and I will set My sanctuary in their midst forevermore. My tabernacle also shall be with them; indeed I will be their God, and they shall be My people. The nations also will know that I, the Lord, sanctify Israel, when my sanctuary is in their midst forevermore.

(Ezekiel 37:24–28)

1. Israel and Judah, cast out but never forgotten.
   Ezekiel 36:16–28
2. The Kingdoms of Israel and Judah restored.
   Daniel 7:27
   Ezekiel 37:11–14
   Ezekiel 39:21-29
   Jeremiah 32:37–41
3. Israel and Judah brought back to serve.
   Ezekiel 37:21–23
   Zechariah 10:6–8
4. "One King," Jesus.
   Ezekiel 37:24–28
   Jeremiah 23:3–8

F. The Sabbath and Millennial Feasts Will Be Observed

The Sabbath was made for man, and not man for the Sabbath. Therefore the Son of Man is also Lord of the Sabbath.

(Mark 2:27–28)

1. Millennial Worship
   Isaiah 2:2-3
   Isaiah 66:18-23
   Zechariah 14:17-21

The observance of Sabbath, or *Shabbat*, was part of the Ten Commandments given to Moses in Exodus 20:8–11 and has been a long time memorial with God and His people.

Jesus observed the Sabbath, but unlike the strict religious rules that Jewish leaders observe, His observation was on the transformation of man's heart in respect to God. Jesus teaches that the Sabbath is to be a blessing to man and not a burden. It is a day of rest and reflection and, most important, a day to keep and honor God.

The Feasts of the Lord play an important part in the Old Testament observance of the Hebrew calendar. Jesus always observed the holy days and the celebrations of His Jewish tradition. According to the forty-fifth chapter of the book of Ezekiel, we will observe two specific feasts during the Millennium. These feasts will reflect the heritage of the Hebrews who now follow Christ, as well as a reminder to Christian believers of the Jewish roots and tradition of our faith.

#1 The Feast of Passover, Pesach and the Feast of Unleavened Bread

> Now the Feast of Unleavened Bread drew near, which is called the Passover.
>
> (Luke 22:1)

The following is a quote from Rabbi Wayne Dosick[53]:

> To today's Jew, the *Feast of Pesach*—with all of its customs, traditions, and observances—is central to Jewish life. It commemorates the Jewish people's being freed from bondage and becoming a nation, and it celebrates the enduring human quest for freedom. It is a holiday with great historical significance and continually unfolding meaning, for within the celebration of historical redemption is the hope and the promise of ultimate redemption. *Pesach L'atid*, the "Passover of the Future," is the time when all humankind will be redeemed to live in freedom and tranquility in a world dominated by justice, filled with compassion, and enveloped in everlasting peace.

The Passover Supper is significant for Christians, as we remember Christ's final moments before He went to the cross. We celebrate Easter and Christ's Resurrection as our point of freedom from the slavery of sin and His victory over death.

#2 The Feast of Tabernacles, or Booths, Sukkot

> (Exodus 23:16b, Deuteronomy 16:13)

> *And it shall come to pass that everyone who is left of all the nations which came against Jerusalem shall go up from year to year to worship the King, the* Lord *of hosts, and to keep the Feast of Tabernacles.*
>
> (Zechariah 14:16)

---

53 Wayne Dosick, *Living Judaism*, p. 174, copyright 1995, HarperCollins.

The Tabernacle (*mishkan*: residence or dwelling place), according to the Old Testament, was the portable dwelling place for the divine presence of God during the forty years of wilderness wandering of His chosen people. There is an annual symbolic observance of *Sukkot,* when people construct temporary booths to symbolize the tents in which they lived under God's protection in the wilderness.

The Feast of Tabernacles was also called the Feast of Ingathering. In the Hebrew tradition, it celebrated the end of the year, when a portion from the autumn harvest and the fruit of the labor of God's people is brought as an offering into God's House. During the Millennium, the nations will bring a share of their harvest as a memorial to Christ's sovereignty and reign.

When reading the book of Ezekiel, we see a description of the temple in Jerusalem during the Millennium. As wonderful as it is, it is still just a temporary replica of what is to come. The Feast of Tabernacles will be celebrated on an annual basis, looking forward to the day when the New Heaven and New Earth are established. It is then that the heavenly chamber, or *chuppah,* will come down, and the eternal abode of God will be with men.

The beautiful thing about these two feasts is that their meaning and importance will be enjoyed by those who are the sons of Abraham as well as those Gentiles who have come to Christ through faith. We will learn to love and honor each other's traditions. The common thread of our faith is united in one person: the Son of Man, Christ.

G. The Great White Throne Judgment: Revelation 20:5–15

> *Now when the thousand years have expired, Satan will be released from his prison and will go out to deceive the nations which are in the four corners of the earth, Gog and Magog, to gather them together to battle, whose number is as the sand of the sea. They went up on the breadth of the earth and surrounded the camp of the saints and the beloved city. And fire came down from God out of heaven and devoured them. The devil, who deceived them, was cast into the lake of fire and brimstone where the beast and the false prophet are. And they will be tormented day and night forever and ever.*
>
> *(Revelation 20: 7–10)*

The final act of rebellion will be near the end of the Millennium, when Satan will be loosed for a season. He will lead many astray. He gathers a second army to bring a second battle. A portion of mankind will follow him in this final rebellion. Gog and Magog represent the leaders of a coalition of

rebellious nations. It is a short war. God sends fire down from heaven. Satan and his followers are defeated and bound.
1. Gog and Magog attack.
   Ezekiel 38:1–6
   Ezekiel 39:1–8

then the Lord knows how to deliver the godly out of temptations and to reserve the unjust under punishment for the day of judgment.
                                                                (2 Peter 2:9)

The ungodly are tightly held *"under punishment,"* like a prison inmate, awaiting their final judgment and sentencing.

Question: What is the second resurrection and what its purpose?

The second resurrection is when the ungodly stand before Christ and are judged at the Great White Throne. This is their final judgment and sentencing. They are given a new physical/spiritual body that is immortal and will live forever and ever in the lake of fire. There is no way out. They suffer the pain of death only to die again. Sin and death have no more place in heaven or on the earth. Both are eternally confined to the fires of hell. The final judgment and restoration are now complete.

1. The second death and the Great White Throne judgment.
   John 5:22–30
   2 Peter 2:9-14
   Revelation 20:11–13
2. Non-believers, along with death, hell, Satan, and the fallen angels, will be cast bodily into the lake of fire.
   Revelation 20:14–15
   Revelation 21:8

Chapter 16

New Heaven and New Earth

The New Heaven and New Earth: Revelation 21:1–22:5

(+1,000 years, Appendix 4)

> *Now I saw a new heaven and a new earth, for the first heaven and the first earth had passed away. Also there was no more sea. Then I, John, saw the holy city, New Jerusalem, coming down out of heaven from God, prepared as a bride adorned for her husband. And I heard a loud voice from heaven saying, "Behold, the tabernacle of God is with men, and He will dwell with them, and they shall be His people. God Himself will be with them and be their God. And God will wipe away every tear from their eyes; there shall be no more death, nor sorrow, nor crying. There shall be no more pain, for the former things have passed away."*
>
> *Then He who sat on the throne said, "Behold, I make all things new." And He said to me, "Write, for these words are true and faithful."*
>
> *And He said to me, "It is done! I am the Alpha and the Omega, the Beginning and the End. I will give of the fountain of the water of life freely to him who thirsts."*
>
> (Revelation 21:1–6)

At the end of the Millennium, there are several events that will have taken place in preparation for the New Heaven and New Earth.

1. All created things are delivered by Christ back into the hands of God the Father.
2. Sin and death are defeated and no longer have dominion over the earth.

3. The New Heaven and New Earth, man's eternal home, are remade by God.
4. Eden is restored. The realm of the physical earth and the heavenly garden become one, as was God's original plan.
5. The New Jerusalem descends from heaven and replaces the old city.
6. God walks with man.

> *By faith we understand that the worlds were framed by the Word of God so that things which are seen were not made of things which are visible.*
> *(Hebrews 11:3)*

Genesis tells us, *"In the beginning God created the heavens and the earth."* The Hebrew word used to describe God here is *Elohim,* the power of God the creator, Father, Son and Holy Ghost. He creates man, "out of the dust of the earth," and, *"breathed into him the breath of life"* (Genesis 2:7). God's desire has always been to meet with man, His highest creation, and to have fellowship with him.

The realm of heaven is currently divided into three parts: the Garden, the Temple, and the New Jerusalem.[54] Each has a distinct purpose.

A. The Garden

The word "Paradise" (in Hebrew, *PaRDeS*) is used as a synonym for the Garden of Eden and comes from the Old Persian word for "walled orchard garden" or "enclosed hunting park."

God resides in the realm of the spirit, and all that was created is in the realm of the physical. It is in Eden where these two realms meet. Eden is called paradise, which also means "the garden of God's delight." In Hebrew, it is called *Gan 'Edhen.* After Adam was cast out, God placed an angel with his flaming sword, to guard the Gates of Eden. In the Hebrew tradition, the Garden is divided into a higher and a lower division. The higher *Gad 'Edhen* is also called the "Garden of Righteousness," and it appears back on earth at the end of time. It also includes the idea that the righteous will be clothed in garments of light and will dance with God in celebration. (Doesn't this sound like the *kittel* and celebration in the Hebrew wedding?) The lower division of Gan' Edhen is called *Gehinniom,* or *Sheol*, which translates into English as hell.

1. Three references to Paradise in the New Testament.
   Luke 23:43
   2 Corinthians 12:4
   Revelation 2:7

---
54 Perry Stone, *Secrets from Beyond the Grave*, p. 81.

2. The word "paradise" (other than Eden) used in the Old Testament.
   Song of Solomon 4:12–15
   Ecclesiastes 2:4–6
   Nehemiah 2:7–8
3. Reference to "Eden Restored" and the inheritance of the righteous.
   Ezekiel 36:33–36
   Ezekiel 47:1–12
   Zechariah 8:11–12

Jesus tells the thief on the cross about God's Paradise. I would suggest that the Bosom of Abraham and Paradise are synonymous. The rebellion and fall of man brought about the separation of the realm of earth from the realm of heaven. The things that are "Holy" (in Hebrew, *Qadosh*), cannot coexist with the unholy.

B. The Temple

The Temple of God, or Throne of God, is where God resides as He reigns over the affairs of heaven and earth. It is the court of heaven. It is a place filled with God's glorious presence. The angels are the ministers of God as they carry out His instructions. Jesus has been sitting at His right hand since the beginning of the Church age. In the Revelation to John the Apostle (Revelation 4:1), John is "caught up" to the heavenly Temple, where he observes heaven's configuration.

1. The Throne and the One who sits upon it.
   Revelation 4:2-3
2. The twenty-four Elders sit as priests.
   Revelation 4:4
3. Seven lamps, the Seven Spirits of God.
   Revelation 4:5
4. Sea of Glass and the Living Creatures.
   Revelation 4:6–11
5. The Golden Altar
   Revelation 8:2–4
6. The Ark of the Covenant.
   Revelation 11:19

Now this is the main point of the things we are saying: We have such a High Priest, who is seated at the right hand of the throne of the Majesty in the heavens, a Minister of the sanctuary and of the true tabernacle which the Lord erected, and not man.

(Hebrews 8:1–2)

After the temporary Tabernacle, there were two Temples built in Jerusalem.[55] The first was built by Solomon in 957 BC and destroyed during the Babylonian captivity in 586 BC. The second temple was built between 538 and 515 BC, enhanced by Herod in 20 BC, and destroyed by the Romans in AD 70. The Dome of the Rock was built on the temple site in AD 691 by followers of Islam. In the 1967 war, the Jewish people recaptured the temple site. Modern Jews would like to rebuild the temple on its original site, but the Dome of the Rock still sits on the site. For the Jews to remove the Islamic shrine would bring an immediate outpouring of rage by their surrounding Arab neighbors.

The beauty of God's plan is in His timing. The Millennial Temple (some call it Ezekiel's Temple) can only be built during the Millennial reign of the Messiah. All these temples are replicas that were and are to serve as reminders of what God's true Temple is about.

When the New Jerusalem comes to earth, there is no longer a need for the Temple as a structure or a place to rule. The heavenly Temple that exists at the present time will be gone. God and the Lamb are the Temple (Revelation 21:22–23).

C. The New Jerusalem, the New Heaven and New Earth

> *Then He who sat on the throne said, "Behold, I make all things new." And He said to me, "Write, for these words are true and faithful."*
> *(Revelation 21:5)*

In Revelation 21:10–21, the City is described with a beauty beyond imagination and measure. The foundation is a square twelve thousand furlongs, or fifteen hundred miles (Revelation 21:16), on a side. Its height is also twelve thousand furlongs. There are two shapes that fit this description. One is a cube, and the second is a pyramid. Biblical scholars fall on both sides of this debate.

Question: Are the New Heaven and New Earth at one location or two?

The New Jerusalem is the City that Christ Himself has been preparing since His ascension into heaven before Pentecost. The Holy City now comes out of its place in heaven and descends to the New Earth. It is the *Holy Chuppah*, which was prepared for His Bride. It is also called the Tabernacle of God, the City of God, the Celestial City, and Heavenly Jerusalem, and it is literally *heaven on earth*. The whole City, which is occupied by the redeemed, is metaphorically called the Bride.

---

55   See appendix 2, "Kingdom History of Israel and Judah."

1. The City in the Old Testament.
   Isaiah 65:17–19
   Isaiah 66:22
2. The City in the New Testament
   Hebrews 1:10–12
   Hebrews 11:9–10
   Hebrews 12:22–24
   Hebrews 13:14
3. The City as the Bride.
   Ephesians 5:25–27
   Revelation 21:2
   Revelation 21:9
4. Only believers will be allowed into the City.
   Isaiah 35:8–10
   Joel 3:17
   Galatians 5:19–21
   Revelation 21:27
5. The City comes to the New Earth as God's eternal residence.
   Revelation 3:12
   Revelation 21:2–3
   Revelation 21:10–21
6. There is no Temple; God and the Lamb are the Temple.
   John 4:21–24
   Revelation 7:15
   Revelation 21:22–26

D. The New Jerusalem, Our Eternal Home

The prophecy of Isaiah 7:14 was fulfilled in Matthew 1:23, when Mary bore Jesus. She was instructed by the angel to call Him Immanuel, *"God with us."* Jesus was God incarnate, that is, God in human form, coming to earth for the redemption of mankind.

Heaven—the new earth—is a physical place where we will dwell with glorified physical bodies (1 Corinthians 15:35–58). The heaven believers will experience will be a new and perfect planet in which to dwell. The new earth will be free from sin, evil, sickness, suffering, and death. Our transformation will be complete. What is holy must never become what is common. Therefore, what is common must become holy. God completes His plan.

The presence of God now comes full circle. God's desire is that, *"all of the earth shall be filled with the glory of the Lord" (Numbers 14:21).* The New Jerusalem is where believers in Christ will spend eternity. God the Father brings His heavenly abode down to earth, and the presence of God is with redeemed mankind. The wall of separation is over.

The New Jerusalem in Hebrew is called *YHWH Shammah*, "the Lord is there." The departed Glory has returned. Jesus, the Son of God, sits at His right side. The Holy City and God will be with man. Paradise is restored. Heaven is open. God will walk with man. The wonders that surround Him will be beyond imagination. He will open His storehouse of blessings upon those He loves. Eternal life will be a never-ending discovery of God's love, grace, and beauty. What God has in mind is more wonderful than we can comprehend. Jesus gives His final invitation in the closing verses of Revelation chapter 22. Can it be any better than this?

> *I Jesus have sent mine angel to testify unto you these things in the churches. I am the Root and the Offspring of David, and the Bright and Morning Star.*
>
> *And the Spirit and the bride say, "Come!" And let him that heareth say, "Come!" And let him who thirsts come. And whosoever will, let him take the water of life freely.*
>
> *For I testify unto every man that heareth the words of the prophecy of this book, If any man shall add unto these things, God shall add unto him the plagues that are written in this book: And if any man shall take away from the words of the book of this prophecy, God shall take away his part out of the book of life, and out of the holy city, and from the things which are written in this book.*
>
> *He which testifies to these things says, "Surely I am coming quickly." Amen. Even so, come, Lord Jesus!*
>
> (Revelation 22:16–20)

Epilogue

The Lord's Treasure

> *This Book of the Law shall not depart from your mouth, but you shall meditate in it day and night, that you may observe to do according to all that is written in it. For then you will make your way prosperous, and then you will have good success. Have I not commanded you? Be strong and of good courage; do not be afraid, nor be dismayed, for the LORD your God is with you wherever you go."*
>
> (Joshua 1:8–9)

Each hour of my devotion to the Bible and composition of this book was framed with prayer and a deep desire and thirst for Him. Many mornings I awoke and the Holy Spirit gave me a fresh perspective on the words and content of what I was to write. This book is still a "work-in-progress," as the Spirit gives direction. I do not understand all of these truths, but like you, I am a seeker of His truth.

Little did I know as I heard the call to write the book in December of 2008, that it would take more than two years to complete. At the same time, my personal struggle with a cancer that was won in 1997 would recur, and I would face many battles over the same two-year period. Many times I was so weak that I was unsure of completing the work, but I was never robbed of the joy the Lord has placed in me and before me. The joy of the Lord is my strength. *"The Lord bless thee and keep thee" (Numbers 6:24).* The word for "keep" in Hebrew is *Shamar*, which means to hedge in, guard, and protect. He has been here with me.

The struggle was no less apparent in March 2010, when the forces against me came to a head. Five years earlier, Linda and I had been called of the Lord to become the prayer champions through an international ministry for a country in south Asia (name omitted to protect the nationals with whom

I work). In December of 2009 I had undergone two serious surgeries for my recurring cancer.

In support of my responsibilities as prayer champion, it has been my desire to travel to south Asia each year to be current on the prayer effort. As the date to leave in late March 2010 approached, my physical strength and condition were not good. As I prayed about the trip, three needs came to my mind. First, of course, was the physical need. The second was that I had not sensed the prayer support of others, which was needed for the trip. Third, I had been asked to assist and train those in the country with their effort to provide clean, safe drinking water. As a retired engineer, these were skills I had not used since the early seventies.

As the departure date of March 30 approached, I knew I needed to make a decision. There were three other men who had also planned on the trip, and I was to act as the team leader. I knew that physically, I should not be going.

When the way is darkest, the Lord always sends in the light. While struggling with the issues on the night of March 15, the Lord came to me in a dream. I saw myself walking toward a large and beautiful all-white sanctuary. As I approached, the doors opened, and standing inside was the Lord. He motioned for me to come in. As I entered the room, it reminded me of a very large vestibule, not unlike what I've seen in many large churches. What was unusual about this vestibule was that it was all white and the floor was covered from one end to another with small white boxes shaped like storage chests. The Lord stood in their midst. He then spoke to me. "Come in. I'm going to allow you to use some of My treasures." He took one of the boxes, opened the lid, and put His hand inside. Then, He reached over to me and placed His hand on my chest. Immediately, a great warmth came over my body. The Lord knew I had been dealing for several weeks with chest and stomach pain accompanied by a great deal of anxiety and demonic attacks. At that instant, I knew the Lord would deliver me physically by His gracious Hand. I awoke the next morning with the knowledge of the Lord's provision for my health and the strength to go on the trip. His instruction was to concentrate on the next one hundred feet and allow His control over all issues beyond one hundred feet.

In contemplation of the travel to Asia, I also knew He would allow me to see many of His treasures. Many miraculous things were about to happen. My part was to be obedient to His call. I was to trust in His strength, and His alone.

God never gives us a vision but what He affirms it! Later that morning, while working about the house, the phone rang. A lady introduced herself as working for the Morris Cerullo Ministry Prayer Line. She was calling during a live television taping session. Their call was totally unexpected. She asked if there were any prayer needs? I conveyed the three requests I had made to the Lord the day before. As we prayed, I knew God had just miraculously provided His answer to the second need on the list. After we had prayed, she said, "Prayer Line will continue to pray for these needs every day for the next thirty days."

As I hung up the phone, my heart was filled with the joy of knowing God's control was being applied to my prayers about the trip. I was reminded of God's instruction to Joshua as he was about to lead the children of Israel into the Promised Land.

The next day, as I was sharing my dream with a brother in the Lord, he asked, "Thirty days ... when does that end?" We got out a calendar and counted from March 16... thirty days ... April 14. You know, April 14 is the exact day of my return from south Asia. God's answer to prayer: to the exact day. How good is our God!

Final Words

Finding God's Treasure

> *Jesus said to them, "Have you understood all these things?" They said to Him, "Yes, Lord." Then He said to them, "Therefore every scribe instructed concerning the kingdom of heaven is like a householder who brings out of his treasure things new and old."*
>
> *(Matthew 13:51–52)*

In the Living Bible, Matthew 13: 52 reads, "*Those experts in Jewish law who are now My disciples have double treasure … from the Old Testament as well as from the New!*"

In our journey together, it has been my desire for you to discover the treasures in God's Word. Each day draws us closer to Him and makes our homeward journey to the Heavenly City one of joy.

As I compose the final lines of *The Groom's Arrival*, I am mindful that He treasures you and I most of all. The plans He has for us are a measure of His great love.

I pray for your journey. Some days it is only one hundred feet at a time, but remember who holds the treasure map. I look forward to the day when we will sit together in heavenly places and reminisce about our travel home. We'll have all the time we need: we'll have an eternity!

If you have not personally experienced the risen Savior, you need to respond to His invitation to come. You are His most valued treasure!

> *And the Spirit and the bride say, "Come!" And let him who hears say, "Come!" And let him who thirsts come. Whoever desires, let him take the water of life freely … The grace of our Lord Jesus Christ be with you all. Amen.*
>
> *(Revelation 22:17, 21)*

John Cooper
February 18, 2011

Notes

Scripture Verses:
New King James Version, copyright 1979, 1980, 1982 by Thomas Nelson, Inc.

References and Footnotes
1. *The Nelson Study Bible* (NKJV), 1997, Thomas Nelson, Inc.
2. *The MacArthur Study Bible* (NKJV), 1997, Word Publishing.
3. *The ESV Study Bible, English Standard Version* (ESV), 2008, Crossway Bibles.
4. Wayne Dosick, *Living Judaism: The Complete Guide to Jewish Belief, Tradition, & Practice*, 1995, HarperCollins Publishers Inc.

Tradition, text boxes
5. Glenn Kay, *Jewish Wedding Customs and the Bride of Messiah*, by Concord Messianic Fellowship, http://www.messianicfellowship.50webs.com/wedding.html (Dec. 5, 2009)
6. Yedidah, *The Ancient Jewish Wedding Ceremony*, www.laydownlife.net/yedidah (Dec. 5, 2009)
7. Sheva Brachot, *The Seven Blessings Recited at a Traditional Jewish Wedding*, Orthodox Union Jewish Wedding Guide, *www.jewish-history.com/minhag.htm*, (April 2, 2009)
8. Richard Booker, *Here Comes the Bride, Jewish Wedding Customs and the Messiah*, Sounds of the Trumpet, Inc., copyright 1995

Chapter 5
Shiddukhin, Selecting a Bride
9. *The ESV Study Bible*, Christ's Edict-letters to the Seven Churches," chart p. 2465

Chapter 6
Mikvah, the Ritual Cleansing
    10. Mark L. Porter, *The History of Baptism from Jewish Ritual to Christian Doctrine,* May 6, 2008,Historical Resources, *http.//historicalresources.suite101.com*, (April 17,2009)

Chapter 10
Eyrusin, the Gifts of the Holy Spirit and How They Work
    11. Don and Katie Fortune, *Discover Your God Given Gifts, copyright 1987,* Chosen Books, Fleming H. Revell Co. Publisher, chapter 1, pp.14–20

Chapter 11
Nisuin, the Presentation, Bema Judgment
    12. J. Hampton Keathley, III, Th.M., *The Doctrine of Rewards: The Judgment Seat (Bema) of Christ,* Bible.org., *http.//www.bible.org/page.php?page_id=407*, (April 11,2009)
    13. Undisclosed Author, *Bema Seat—Rewards,* All About God Ministries Inc. *http://www. allaboutgod.com/bema-seat.htm,* (April 11,2009)

Chapter 12
Chuppah, Jesus Opens the Scroll
    14. John Walvoord, *The Revelation of Jesus Christ,* Copyright 1966 by The Moody Bible Institute of Chicago
    15. Undisclosed Author, *Abaddon/ Apollyon/Apollo,* Bible Prophesy Research, November 12, 1998, *http://philologos.org/bpr/files/a009.htm,* (August 26, 2009)

Chuppah, Jesus Opens the Scroll/Days of Daniel
    16. Dr. Alva J. McClain, *Daniel's Prophecy of the Seventy Weeks*, copyright 1940, 1969, Zondervan Publishing House, Grand Rapids, Michigan

Chuppah, Satan Is Cast out of Heaven
    17. *The MacArthur Study Bible*, commentary on the twenty-three hundred days of Daniel 8:14, page 1241.

Chuppah, the Tribulation Harvest
    18. Henry Alford, *The Greek New Testament, IV,* pp. 690–691.
    19. John Walvoord , *The Prophecy Knowledge Handbook,* p. 392.
    20. James A. Patch, *Harvest,* Study Light, The International Standard Bible Encyclopedia, *http.//www.studylight.org/enc/isb/view.cgi?number=T4127*

***Chuppah*, the Day of the Lord**
    21. *The MacArthur Study Bible*, footnote on Isaiah 2:12 , p. 958.

Chapter 14
***Seudas Mitzvah*, the Marriage Supper**
    22. Lambert Dolphin, *The Marriage Supper of the Lamb,*, August 23, 1993, *http://ldolphin.org/Msup.html,*(April 11,2009)
    23. G. W. Finley, *The Marriage Supper of the Lamb* , End Time Pilgrim Ministries, *http://www.endtimepilgrim.org/marriage.htm,* (April 11, 2009)

Chapter 15
The Sabbath and Millennial Feasts
    24. Wayne Dosick, *Living Judaism: The Complete Guide to Jewish Belief, Tradition, & Practice*, 1995, HarperCollins Publishers, Inc., p. 174.

appendix 1: The Seven Blessings of Revelation
The Nelson Study Bible, Notes on Revelation 1:3, p. 2164

appendix 2: Kingdom History of Israel and Judah
The Nelson Study Bible, Chart, pp. 620–621

appendix 1: The Seven Blessings of Revelation

B#1 **Blessed is he who reads, hears and keeps**
Blessed is he who reads and those who hear the words of this prophecy, and keep those things which are written in it; for the time is near. (Revelation 1:3)

B#2 **Blessed is he who dies in Christ**
Then I heard a voice from heaven saying to me, "Write: 'Blessed are the dead who die in the Lord from now on.'" "Yes," says the Spirit, "that they may rest from their labors, and their works follow them." (Revelation 14:13)

B#3 **Blessed is he who watches and keeps his garments**
Behold, I am coming as a thief. Blessed is he who watches, and keeps his garments, lest he walk naked and they see his shame. (Revelation 16:15)

B#4 **Blessed is he who is invited to the marriage supper**
Then he said to me, "Write: 'Blessed are those who are called to the marriage supper of the Lamb!'" And he said to me, "These are the true sayings of God." (Revelation 19:9)

B#5 **Blessed is he who has a part in the first resurrection**
And they lived and reigned with Christ for a thousand years. But the rest of the dead did not live again until the thousand years were finished. This is the first resurrection. Blessed and holy is he who has part in the first resurrection. Over such the second death has no power, but they shall be priests of God and of Christ, and shall reign with Him a thousand years. (Revelation 20:4b–6)

B#6. **Blessed is he who keeps the Words**
Then he said to me, "These words are faithful and true." And the Lord God of the holy prophets sent His angel to show His servants the things which must shortly take place. "Behold, I am coming quickly! Blessed is he who keeps the words of the prophecy of this book." (Revelation 22:6–7)

B#7. **Blessed are those who do His commandments**
Blessed are those who do His commandments, that they may have the right to the tree of life, and may enter through the gates into the city. (Revelation 22:14)

appendix 2: Kingdom History of Israel and Judah

To understand God's plan for Israel, one must understand its history. A study of the kingdom history of Israel can be divided into six eras. The future seventh and eighth era will occur after Christ's return:

1. **United Kingdom** (1043–931 BC)
   All twelve tribes were under a common leadership, ending with the reign of the Kings Saul, David, and Solomon. The first Temple is built.

2. **Divided Kingdom** (931–722 BC)
   At the end of Solomon's reign, the kingdom was divided (I Kings 12:1–II Kings 17:41) into two separate nations: the ten northern tribes comprising Israel and the two southern tribes comprising Judah and Benjamin. In 721 BC, Israel was conquered by Assyria (II Kings 16:1–17:41) and dispersed among foreign nations. Theologians have coined the phrase, "The ten lost tribes of Israel."

3. **Surviving Kingdom of Judah** (721–605 BC)
   Judah and Benjamin continue to exist as a nation until the time of the Babylonian captivity, which began in 605 BC. The dispersion of the people took place between 605 and 586 BC. In a sense because of their disobedience to God, they are returned to state of slavery (Jeremiah 2:14–25) not unlike their former slavery in Egypt. The seventy years of exile lasted from 605 BC to 536 BC.

4. **Rebuilt Kingdom of Judah** (536 BC–AD 70)
   The decree of Cyrus, king of Persia in 536 BC (II Chronicles 36:22–23), is issued, and Zerubbabel returns in 538 BC, followed by Ezra in 458 BC and Nehemiah in 445 BC. The rebuilding of the temple and the walls of Jerusalem are completed, along with the reinstitution of the Law.

5. **Dispersed Kingdom of Judah** (AD 70–1948 AD)
   Rome sent her armies into the land of Judah in AD 66. By AD 70, they had sacked, burned, and dispersed the people. The second temple was destroyed, and the land was completely occupied by Rome. From AD 70 until 1948 Israel, did not exist as a nation but continued to maintain their religious heritage.

6. **Reinstated Kingdom of Judah** (1948 to the present)
   On May 14, 1948, the United Nations decreed and established Palestine (Israel) to be the national homeland for the Jewish people. These are a people who have lived almost two thousand years without a nation and yet maintained a national identity. The miracle of dispersal and being re-gathered in their homeland is a fulfillment of God's promises through His prophets.

7. **The Millennial Kingdom** (future)

8. **The New Heaven and New Earth** (future)

appendix 3 The Hebrew Wedding Tradition and the Return of Christ

Jesus Seeks a Bride:
Choson, the Groom
Kallah, the Bride

Hebrew Tradition	*Shiddukhin,* Seeking a True Bride	*Mikvah,* Ritual Cleansing	*Mohar,* Bride Price	*Matan,* Bridal Gift	*Ketubah,* Marriage Covenant signed	*The Groom* Returns home to prepare a place	*Eyrusin,* The Betrothal, Bride's preparation
New Covenant	Jesus' Incarnation and Ministry	Repentance and Baptism	Crucifixion & the Payment for Sin	Pentecost and the Holy Spirit	Christ's New Covenant	Ascension of Christ	The Church Age and the work of the Holy Spirit

Nisuin, Bride's "capture" and presentation	*Chuppah,* Bridal Chamber and Ceremony	*Ketubah,* Marriage Covenant Authenticated	*An Inheritance,* The Father's Gift	*Yichud,* The Seclusion	*Seudas Mitzvah,* The Marriage Supper
"Rapture" of the Church. Tribulation starts	Heaven "sealed", Marriage of the Lamb begins	Who is Worthy?	The Scroll and the Tribulation Harvest	The Bride is Glorified	The End of the Age, Celebration in Heaven

Millennial Reign of Christ → New Heaven and New Earth

Revised by John Cooper 12/24/10

appendix 4 — The Olivet Discourse, Days of Daniel, and Jesus' Scroll

Day -1,260			Day 0			Day +1,260		Day +1,290
#1 Pre-Tribulation, Church Age	#2 Tribulation	#3 Abomination of Desolation*	#4 Great Tribulation	#5 Tribulation Harvest	#6 Wrath of God	#7 Day of the Lord		#8 The Earth is Cleansed

Jesus' Olivet Discourse, Matthew Chapters 24–25

| Matthew 24:4–8 | Matthew 24:9–14 | Matthew 24:15 | Matthew 24:16–21 | Matthew 24:36–44; Matthew 13:24–30; Matthew 13:37–40 | Matthew 24:22 | Matthew 24: 27–31 | Matthew 24:45-51; Matthew 13:40–43; Matthew 13:47–50 |

Days of Daniel, Book of Daniel

| Daniel 2:28-30; Daniel 8:15–22; Daniel 9:24-26 | Daniel 2:40-43; Daniel 7:7-8; Daniel 7:19; Daniel 10:14 | Daniel 7:20; Daniel 9:27; Daniel 11:29-31; Daniel 11:36–39; Daniel 12:11 | Daniel 7:21; Daniel 7:23–25; Daniel 12:1; Daniel 12:6–7 | Daniel 3:26-28; Daniel 11:32–35; Daniel 12:10 | Daniel 2:44-45; Daniel 7:11–12; Daniel 12:2-3 | Daniel 2:34-35; Daniel 7:13; Daniel 7:22; Daniel 12:11 | Daniel 7:15-18; Daniel 7:26–27 |

Jesus' Scroll, Book of Revelation

| Rev. C2; Rev. C3 | Rev. C6; Rev. C13 | Rev. 12:7–13 | Rev. C8–C9; Rev. C11–C13; Rev. 12:6; Rev. 13:5 | Rev. C7; Rev. C11; Rev. C14 | Rev. C15; Rev. 16:1–14 | Rev. 16:15–21; Rev. C17; Rev. C18; Rev. 19:11–16 | Rev. 19:17–18; Rev. 20:3 |

Day +1,291 → **#9, The Marriage of The Lamb** — Matthew 25:1-13; Matthew 22:2–14; Rev. 19:1–10

Day +1,334 → **#10, Millennial Reign of Christ, Day +1,335, 1,000 yrs.** — Matthew 25:14–46; Daniel 12:12–13; Daniel 7:14; Revelation 20:4–15

→ **#11, New Heaven and New Earth, +1,000 Years** — Revelation C 21; Revelation 22:1–5

* 1 Maccabees 1:44-64.

Revised by John Cooper 1/15/11

appendix 5: Ten Elements of the Hebrew Wedding Tradition

1. ***Shiddukhin*, Selecting a Bride**
   This is the first step in the marriage process prior to the betrothal. For devout Jews, it is common for the father of the groom to employ a *shadkhan,* or matchmaker, in the process of bride selection.

2. ***Mikveh*, the Ritual Cleansing**
   Prior to his encounter with the prospective bride, both the groom and the bride-to-be would have undergone the separate ritual cleansing or immersion.

3. ***Mohar*, the Bride Price**
   The groom would pay a dowry to the bride's family.

4. ***Ketubah*, the Marriage Contract**
   The word *ketubah* means written. The Marriage Covenant includes the conditions of the marriage contract and the promises made by the groom to the bride and her family.

5. ***Matan***, **the Bridal Gift**
   At the time of the groom's departure, he would give his wife-to-be the betrothal ring as a pledge of his love. The gift was to serve as a reminder to her during their days of separation.

6. ***Eyrusin*, the Betrothal**
   The word *kinddushin* stands for the time period of the betrothal and means sanctification or set apart. On his return home, the groom begins the task of adding rooms (*chador,* chambers) to His father's house. In Hebrew tradition, the betrothal period could be a year or more.

7. ***Nisuin*, the Presentation**
   The word *nisuin* means to lift up or carry. After completion of the new home and at a time determined by the groom's father, the groom and his friends would assemble and proceed to the bride's parents' home. The bride would not know the day or time of his return. The groom's procession would usually start at dusk with torches, shouts, and trumpets (*shofar*) leading them across the hillsides. He would claim his bride and return by processional to his home for the marriage ceremony.

8. ***Chuppah*, Bridal Chamber and Ceremony**
   The formal ceremony was to be held under the temporary canopy or *chuppah*. The words of the ceremony are taken from Psalm 45 and Isaiah 61:10–Isaiah 62:5. These are the traditional vows of love as expressed in God's love for Israel. After reading the scripture, they sign the *ketubah* and seal it with the sharing of a cup of wine called the Cup of Acceptance.

9. ***Yichud*, the Seclusion**
   At the end of the ceremony, the bride and groom go into the actual *chuppah* for a time of seclusion called *yichud*. The door to the wedding chamber is closed and locked from the inside. The groom's friend stands guard outside.

10. ***Seudas Mitzvah*, the Marriage Supper**
    The Marriage Supper is held at the end of the *Yichud*. The guests participate in the *seudas mitzvah*, or *L'sameach choson v' kallah*, to celebrate in joy with the new couple as they start their married life.

> *"But the end of all things is at hand; therefore be serious and watchful in your prayers."*
> *1 Peter 4:7*